ALLIGATORS AND CROCODILES

Great Creatures of the World

ALLIGATORS AND CROCODILES

Facts On File

New York • Oxford • Sydney

Alligators and Crocodiles
A Great Creatures of the World book

Facts On File, Inc.   Facts On File Limited
460 Park Avenue South or Collins Street
New York NY 10016   Oxford OX4 1XJ
USA   United Kingdom

Jonathan Scott/Planet Earth Pictures

Written by Lesley Dow

Adapted from material supplied by:

Dr Angel C. Alcala, professor of biology and director,
Marine Laboratory, Silliman University, Philippines

David K. Blake, warden, St Lucia Crocodile Centre,
Natal Parks Board, South Africa

Peter Brazaitis, assistant curator, Animal Department,
Central Park Zoo, New York Zoological Society, New
York, USA

Dr Eric Buffetaut, director of research, Centre
National de la Recherche Scientifique, University of
Paris, France

Dr Mark W. J. Ferguson, head of department of Cell
and Structural Biology, University of Manchester,
United Kingdom

Dr Stephen Garnett, consultant biologist and science
journalist, Blackwood, Victoria, Australia

Dr Leonard Ginsburg, assistant director, Vertebrate
Paleontology, Museé Nationale d'Histoire Naturelle,
Paris, France

Tommy C. Hines, consultant on alligator and croco-
dilian management, Florida, USA

Dr Dale R. Jackson, research zoologist, Florida
Natural Areas Inventory, The Nature Conservancy,
Florida, USA

Dr Jeffrey W. Lang, associate professor, Department
of Biology, University of North Dakota, USA

Dr William Ernest Magnusson, research scientist,
Instituto Nacional de Pesquisas de Amazônia, Brazil

Greg Mitchell, project manager, Mainland Holdings
Crocodile Farm, Lae, Papua New Guinea

J. T. Victor Onions, project manager, Edward River
Crocodile Farm, Cairns, Queensland, Australia

A. C. (Tony) Pooley, consultant on crocodile farming,
conservation, and education, Scottburgh, South Africa

Charles A. Ross, museum specialist, Department of
Vertebrate Zoology, National Museum of Natural
History, Smithsonian Institution, Washington, DC,
USA

Dr John Shield, veterinarian, Cairns, Australia

Dr Laurence Taplin, zoologist, Queensland National
Parks and Wildlife Service, Australia

Dave Taylor, alligator research project coordinator,
Louisiana Department of Wildlife and Fisheries, USA

Dr G. W. Trompf, associate professor and head,
Department of Religious Studies, University of
Sydney, Australia

Romulus Whitaker, director, Madras Crocodile Bank,
Madras, India

Dr Zhou Guoxing, deputy director, Beijing Natural
History Museum and vice-chairman, Chinese Associ-
ation of Natural Science Museums, Beijing, People's
Republic of China

Dr George R. Zug, curator, Division of Amphibians
and Reptiles, National Museum of Natural History,
Smithsonian Institution, Washington, DC, USA

Produced by
Weldon Owen Pty Limited,
43 Victoria Street, McMahons Point, NSW 2060
Telex AA 23038 Fax (02) 929 8352
A member of the Weldon International Group
of Companies   Sydney • San Francisco • Hong Kong
• London • Chicago

Publisher: John Owen
Publishing Manager: Stuart Laurence
Managing Editor: Beverley Barnes
Project Coordinator: Claire Craig
Picture Editor: Annette Crueger
Designer: Diane Quick
Maps: Greg Campbell
Illustrations: Tony Pyrzakowski
Production Director: Mick Bagnato

Typeset by Keyset Phototype
Printed by Kyodo-Shing Loong Printing Industries
Printed in Singapore

10 9 8 7 6 5 4 3 2 1

Facts On File books are available at special discounts
when purchased in bulk quantities for businesses,
associations, institutions or sales promotions. Please
contact the Special Sales Department of our New York
office at 212/683-2244 (dial 800/322-8755 except in
NY, AK & HI or in Oxford at 0865 728399

Library of Congress Cataloguing-in-Publication Data:
Dow, Lesley.
    Alligators and crocodiles.
    p. cm. — (Great creatures of the world)
    Includes bibliographical references.
    Summary: Discusses the biological features of
alligators and crocodiles, their habitats, lifestyles, and
history.
    ISBN 0-8160-2273-9.
    1. Alligators – Juvenile literature. 2. Crocodiles –
Juvenile literature. [1. Alligators. 2. Crocodiles.] I.
Title. II. Series.
QL666.C9D69 1990   90-31570
597.98—dc20   CIP-AC

A British CIP catalogue record for this book is
available from the British Library.

Page 1: An American alligator hatchling.
Page 2: Even hatchlings can float . . . without being taught.
Opposite page: An adult Nile crocodile bares his teeth.

Australian Picture Library

Anthony Bannister/NHPA

Contents

Jane Burton/Bruce Coleman Ltd

T. Pooley

Jack Green/Australian Nature Photographs

Gerald Cubitt/Bruce Coleman Ltd

Donn Renn/Bruce Coleman Ltd

Opposite page: An American alligator leaps for a tasty morsel — a young egret.

What are alligators and crocodiles?

Alligators, crocodiles, and their less well-known relatives, caimans and gharials, all belong to the same family. There are 22 different *species* in this family and, like all related groups, they have many features in common.

F. Prenzel/Australian Picture Library

What do they have in common?
Alligators, crocodiles, caimans, and gharials are *reptiles*. They belong to the same class of animals as lizards, snakes, and turtles. Like all reptiles they are cold-blooded (or *poikilothermic*, if you want to impress your friends). This means that their body temperature moves up and down according to the temperature of their environment. They have no fur, feathers, or hair to keep them warm, nor do they shiver when they are cold. Like all reptiles they are also *vertebrates*; that is, they have a backbone or spinal column.

Alligators, crocodiles, caimans, and gharials are also *amphibious* — they spend part of their lives in water and part on dry land. They need land, where they *bask* and nest, as much as they need water, where they mate and feed.

Caimans, crocodiles, and gharials live in the *tropics*, where the weather is hot all year round.

They are found in Central and South America, Africa, the Indian subcontinent, Southeast Asia, and northern Australia. Only alligators seem to be able to survive the temperate (warm) climates outside the tropics. However, fossils of their now-*extinct* ancestors have been discovered in all the continents of the world except Antarctica. Remains of these ancient ancestors have been found in Europe, the Soviet Union, Canada, and other countries where no alligators or crocodiles live today. Some of these ancestors were plant-eaters, unlike today's living species.

▲ *Even a tiny mud "island" is big enough for a number of alligators to bask in the warmth of the sun.*

Group name
"Alligators, crocodiles, caimans, and gharials" is quite a mouthful. It is also quite an eyeful for you to read. Most books, including this one, use the group name "alligators and crocodiles" to describe all of them. But remember that whenever you read "alligators and crocodiles" in this book, it also includes their relatives the caimans and gharials.

▼ *Alligator and crocodile nostrils are set in a round disc at the end of the snout so that they can still breathe when the rest of the body is underwater.*

Philip Quirk/Wildlight Photo Agency

Living alligators, crocodiles, caimans, and gharials are *carnivores*, that is, they eat flesh not plants. They are all skilled, stealthy hunters. Their teeth, jaws, and stomachs are designed to catch and digest food of all sizes from insects and snails to fish, birds, and mammals. In fact they will eat almost anything that swims in, wades through, flies over, or comes too near the water they live in ... if it is easy to catch.

Females are usually smaller than males of the same species. They build nests in mounds or holes on land. In these nests they lay one *clutch* of eggs each year. They are "good" mothers. They guard their nests fiercely and look after their hatchlings for some time after they are born.

Alligators, crocodiles, caimans, and gharials are also sociable and gather together in groups to breed and feed. They even "talk" to each other using grunts, coughs, and roars. But they are not always friendly toward each other (especially the males) since they are also very competitive.

▼ *The young Nile crocodile (top) is carnivorous, as an unlucky frog discovered. The adult Indian mugger (bottom) has a large mouth and can eat much bigger prey than a frog.*

Most alligators, crocodiles, caimans, and gharials are timid and slip away quietly when humans approach. There are only three or four species that are big enough and fierce enough to attack and eat humans. But throughout history, humans have pictured these reptiles in stories, paintings, and sculptures as awesome creatures to be treated with great caution and respect, or with fear.

Their fate in our hands

Humans have hunted alligators, crocodiles, caimans, and gharials for their meat or skins ever since the human "newcomers" first began to share the same environment. Humans have also destroyed large areas of *rainforest* and polluted the waters where alligators, crocodiles, caimans, and gharials live and breed. Many species are now in danger of extinction after surviving for some 200 million years.

In recent years, people and governments have realized that we must protect our natural environment and the animals that live there. National parks, where native animals can roam free, and farms and ranches, where alligators, crocodiles, caimans, and gharials can be raised in captivity, may help to protect those that remain in the wild. All alligators, crocodiles, caimans, and gharials are now protected from overhunting by international laws.

If *conservation* is successful you will be able to show your children these magnificent animals alive instead of showing them a stuffed museum specimen of an animal that used to live in the world when you were a child.

Which is which?

The 22 species of alligators, croco-diles, caimans, and gharials are usually divided into three separate groups.

Alligators and caimans

Alligators and caimans belong in one group. An alligator and a caiman are more closely related to each other than either is to a crocodile or a gharial. Alligators and caimans usually have shorter, broader snouts than crocodiles or gharials. Their lower teeth fit into pits in the upper jaw so that you cannot see any lower teeth when their mouths are closed. The largest tooth in their mouths is the fourth tooth in the upper jaw.

If they are so closely related, what is the difference between an alligator and a caiman? Caimans are usually smaller than alligators and have bonier ridges (or "spectacles") between their eyes than alligators. But one species of caiman grows to be as big as or bigger than an alligator, and two species of caiman have no "spectacles." The easiest way to tell alligators and caimans apart is by the country they come from. If you are in the United States or China, the alligator-like animal you see in the wild is a true alligator. If you are in Central or South America, the alligator-like animal you see is in fact a caiman.

▲ *The American alligator's lower teeth cannot be seen when its mouth is closed.*

D. Parer and E. Parer-Cook/Auscape International

◄ American alligators are at home in a wide variety of different habitats.

Adrian Warren/Ardea London

▲ Nile crocodiles have slender snouts, almost no forehead, and a lower tooth that fits into a special notch outside the upper jaw.

Joyce Wildon/Seaphot Limited/Planet Earth Pictures

Crocodiles

Crocodiles belong to the second group. There are more species of crocodiles than there are of alligators, caimans, and gharials put together. Crocodiles have more slender snouts than alligators or caimans. They have a less obvious "forehead" since their snouts merge more smoothly into their skulls. Most of their lower teeth fit into pits in the upper jaw, but the fourth lower tooth fits into a notch on the outside of the upper jaw and can be seen when the mouth is closed. Their largest tooth is the fifth tooth in the upper jaw.

Gharials

There is only one living species of gharial, and it belongs in a group by itself. Gharials have long, thin snouts that are sharply marked off by a sort of "forehead" from the rest of the skull. Their teeth are small and even, and they interlock neatly when the mouth is closed.

If you ever go to an alligator or crocodile farm, look at the animals' heads, snouts, and teeth (but not too closely!) to see if you can tell which is which.

What's in a name?

Which of the three groups does the mugger belong to? Its alternative name is marsh crocodile, and this tells you immediately that it is a crocodile. The false gharial, however, is even more confusing. Its name tells you that it must look like a gharial but it is, in fact, a crocodile. All the other species have names that tell you which group they belong to.

▼ The long thin snout armed with neat sharp teeth makes the gharial an easy species to recognize.

Mike Price/Bruce Coleman Ltd

Ancient alligators and crocodiles

The history of alligators and crocodiles goes back over 200 million years — human history goes back only one million years. Ancient alligators and crocodiles lived at the same time as the dinosaurs but, unlike the dinosaurs, descendants of these ancient alligators and crocodiles have survived to the present day.

▼ *Scientists believe that protosuchians, the original alligator and crocodile ancestors, probably looked like this.*

Tracing their history

There were three main stages in the *evolution* of alligators and crocodiles. The original ancestors, called protosuchians, flourished in the Late Triassic and Early Jurassic (215–200 million years ago). The next stage or group, the mesosuchians, lived from the Jurassic to the Tertiary (200–65 million years ago). The last stage or group, the eusuchians, have lived from the Cretaceous (80 million years ago) to the present day.

▼ *This fossil alligator is considered modern — it is only 80 million years old!*

Did you know?

When the first alligator and crocodile ancestors were alive, the map of the world looked very different from the way it does today. All the continents of the world were joined together in one huge "supercontinent" called Pangaea. As Pangaea split up, new oceans separated groups of alligators and crocodiles from each other. Groups that had once looked very alike began to develop on different continents and in different ways.

American Museum of Natural History

Scientists can identify these three stages by looking at what is called the *secondary bony palate*. In living alligators and crocodiles the secondary bony palate in the roof of the mouth is long, and the internal (inside) nostrils are pushed back some distance from the external (outside) nostrils on the tip of the snout. This allows alligators and crocodiles to breathe through their nostrils, even when their mouths are open underwater. Their ancient relatives had a much shorter secondary bony palate, and the internal and external nostrils were closer together. By looking carefully at the position of the nostrils and the length of the bony palate, scientists can decide which stage the fossils belong to and so how old they are likely to be.

Scientists also look closely at the vertebrae. In protosuchians and mesosuchians, the vertebrae were shaped like spools; that is, both ends of the vertebrae were concave (dented inward). In more recent times, the eusuchians developed vertebrae that were concave at the front and convex (rounded) at the back. The rounded end fits into the front of the vertebra behind it like a ball-and-socket joint.

Protosuchians (215–200 million years ago)

The first alligator and crocodile ancestors were land animals. They did not live partly in the water like today's species. Because they were land animals they had long legs to make walking on land easier. They had shorter snouts than alligators and crocodiles today since they did not need to breathe underwater to catch fish. They were small, probably no more than 3 feet (1 m) long, and looked rather like lizards. They had bony armor with two rows of plates along the back and tail, and a belly shield as well. They had a short secondary bony palate and spool-shaped vertebrae.

Mesosuchians (200–65 million years ago)

The oldest mesosuchian fossil found so far is 190 million years old. The mesosuchians had a longer secondary bony palate than their ancestors the protosuchians, but most still had spool-shaped vertebrae. Unlike protosuchians, most of the mesosuchians lived in the sea. They had long snouts and many piercing teeth, which were good for catching and eating fish and other sea creatures. Some mesosuchians probably still came back onto land to lay their eggs, but others developed flippers in place of legs and would have found it difficult to walk on land at all.

▼ *As alligators and crocodiles evolved, the shape of the vertebrae and the length of the secondary bony palate changed.*

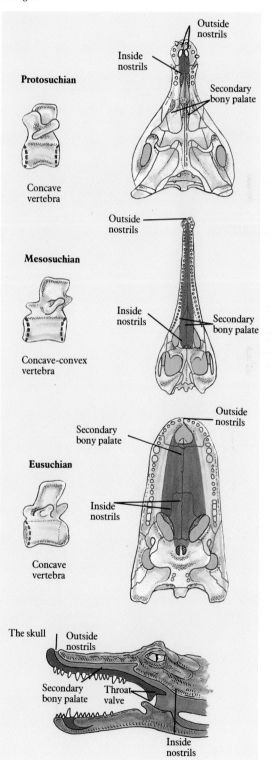

How did they survive?

About 65 million years ago scientists believe that either a meteorite struck the earth or a huge volcano erupted. Many species of land animals (including dinosaurs) and many sea animals became extinct. But freshwater animals such as alligators and crocodiles survived. Perhaps their food supplies were less affected by the disaster than the land plants or marine plankton on which the extinct animals depended.

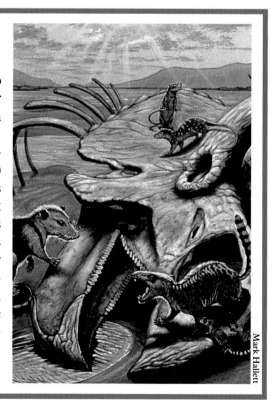

Mark Hallett

Like the evolution of most animals, there are always exceptions to the general rule, and some mesosuchian families were definitely land animals with long legs and short snouts. Some of them even had teeth like dinosaurs and they probably competed with dinosaurs for food.

Eusuchians (80 million years ago to today)

Eusuchians have long secondary palates and ball-and-socket vertebrae. They became dominant about 80 million years ago. Some eusuchians had dinosaur-like teeth and hoofed toes and were most likely land animals, but families in this group are now extinct. Other extinct eusuchian families had long snouts and looked rather like very primitive gharials but, unlike living gharials, they lived in the sea not in fresh water.

Although their land-dwelling and sea-dwelling ancestors are now extinct, 22 species of amphibious, freshwater alligators and crocodiles have survived to the present day. They have managed to outlive their dinosaur relatives through a number of geological and biological upheavals in the Earth's history. We are lucky to have these last survivors of the great age of reptiles.

◀ *Alligators and crocodiles today have armor similar to that of their ancestors, but they have much shorter legs than many of their ancestors.*

Ian Beames/Ardea London

▼ *Most fossil mesosuchians had long snouts and sharp teeth that were perfect for catching fish.*

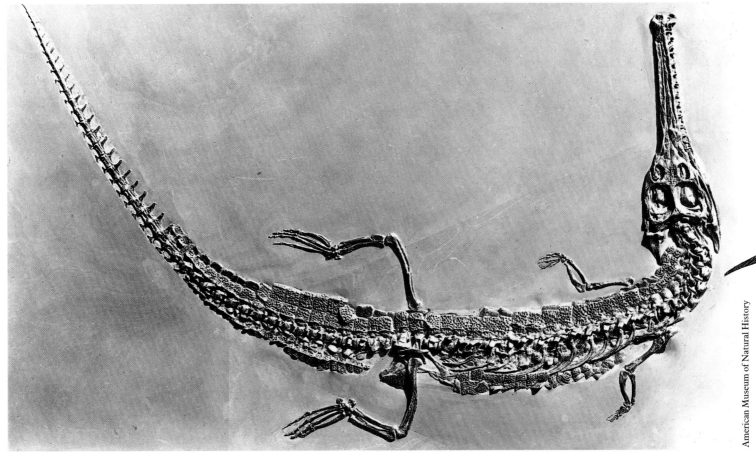

American Museum of Natural History

A crocodile's ankle | **A typical reptile's ankle**
S-shaped joint | Straight joint

To twist and swivel

Most reptiles (and dinosaurs) have an ankle joint that passes in a straight line between the upper and lower rows of ankle bones. Alligators, crocodiles, and their extinct relatives (except the dinosaurs) have an unusual S-shaped angle joint. The joint passes between two small bones that fit together like a peg into a socket. This joint allows the foot to swivel and twist when the animal walks.

▼ ▶ *It is hard to imagine that birds could be related to alligators and crocodiles, until you look at the extinct bird (below). It has some alligator-like features as well as some features of the living secretary bird (right).*

▶ *This simplified "family tree" shows how long ago crocodiles and alligators began to evolve differently from dinosaurs and birds.*

Relatives — extinct and living

The original ancestors of alligators and crocodiles evolved from a group of animals called *thecodontians*. Other groups of animals also evolved from this same group. It is a bit like you sharing a great-great-great-great grandparent with someone else — you are related, but only very distantly.

Ancient relatives

The closest relatives of ancient crocodiles and alligators were the sphenosuchians. They had long legs and short claws, which suggests that they were fast-moving land *predators*.

The next closest relatives, the rauisuchians, were the ruling land carnivores before dinosaurs appeared on the scene. They grew to 20 feet (6 m) in length and had blade-like teeth with serrated edges (like the blade of a steak knife) to grasp and cut prey. They had two rows of small bony plates on their backs.

Another group of relatives, the aetosaurs, had bodies that were almost completely covered by a bony, spiky armor. Their teeth were fairly blunt, and they had no teeth at all at the tip of the snout or in the lower jaw. They must have been plant-eaters not carnivores … despite their fearsome appearance.

The phytosaurs were more distant relatives of ancient alligators and crocodiles. They looked rather like them, but their external nostrils were in front of their eyes not on the tip of their long snouts.

Dinosaurs were very distant relatives of alligators and crocodiles. Lizard-hipped dinosaurs were either carnivorous dinosaurs that walked on their hind legs and ranged in size from 3 feet (1 m) to 50 feet (15 m), or very large plant-eating dinosaurs that walked on all four legs.

Living relatives

Although it may surprise you, alligators and crocodiles are more closely related to birds than to any other living species. Birds, alligators, and crocodiles have a long outer ear canal, a muscular gizzard that grinds up food, and a heart that is separated into four chambers. They all build nests out of plant material and are caring parents. Somewhere in their long evolutionary history they probably shared a common ancestor.

The next closest living relatives of alligators and crocodiles are the scaly lizards whose skin is covered by overlapping horny scales. The tuatara of New Zealand as well as lizards and snakes belong to this group. The scaly lizards, alligators, and crocodiles all have two large openings on each cheek to allow space for their bulging jaw-closing muscles.

Hans Reinhard/Bruce Coleman Ltd

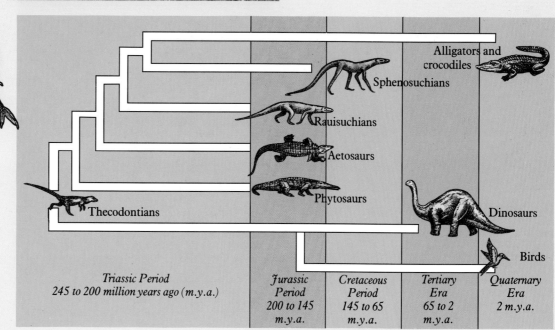

| *Triassic Period* *245 to 200 million years ago (m.y.a.)* | *Jurassic Period* *200 to 145 m.y.a.* | *Cretaceous Period* *145 to 65 m.y.a.* | *Tertiary Era* *65 to 2 m.y.a.* | *Quaternary Era* *2 m.y.a.* |

Kinds of alligators and crocodiles

Living alligators and crocodiles come in all sizes and colors from the 23-foot (7 m) long, gray saltwater crocodile to the 5-foot (1.5 m) long, reddish-brown, Cuvier's dwarf caiman. In this chapter we shall look at similarities and differences among the 22 species of alligators and crocodiles.

American alligator

American alligators are found in the southeastern United States from North Carolina to Southern Florida and from the Atlantic Ocean as far west as Texas. They have wider, longer snouts than their cousins the Chinese alligators and have few or no *osteoderms* (bony buttons) on their bellies.

Chinese alligator

Chinese alligators are only half the size of American alligators and are much more timid. Now found only in the lower Yangtze River of China, Chinese alligators have slightly upturned snouts, a bony plate on their eyelids, and osteoderms on their bellies.

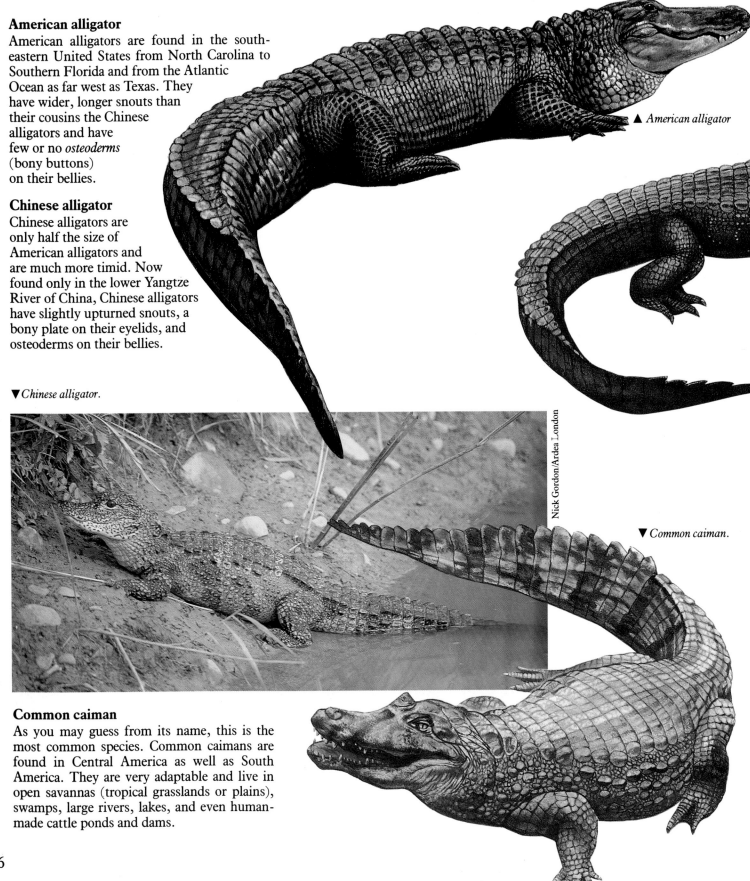

▲ *American alligator*

▼ *Chinese alligator.*

Nick Gordon/Ardea London

▼ *Common caiman.*

Common caiman

As you may guess from its name, this is the most common species. Common caimans are found in Central America as well as South America. They are very adaptable and live in open savannas (tropical grasslands or plains), swamps, large rivers, lakes, and even human-made cattle ponds and dams.

16

▼ *Broad-snouted caiman.*

Broad-snouted caiman

Broad-snouted caimans have the wide, rounded heads typical of swamp-dwelling species although they are sometimes found around the edges of lakes and large rivers as well as swamps.

Black caiman

Black caimans, with their gray-brown heads and black bodies, which are sometimes patterned with white dots, are very colorful. They are the largest caimans and live in flooded forests around lakes and slow-flowing rivers.

Schneider's dwarf caiman

This very abundant species has large, sharp *scutes* (scales that stick out). It is difficult to hold if it struggles. It also has a unique tail, which is very bony and less flexible than the tails of other species. The tail is flat on the top and bottom (the tails of all other species have flattened sides). The tail scutes stick out to the side, making the tail appear even broader.

Schneider's dwarf caimans do not like the open and are usually found in tiny streams in dense rainforest. They rarely bask in the sun. They spend a great deal of time on land sheltering in hollow logs or under fallen debris.

Cuvier's dwarf caiman

Cuvier's dwarf caimans have unusual skulls — high and smooth, rather like a dog's skull. They are the smallest species. Like Schneider's dwarf caimans, they do not like open spaces — but nor do they like dense rainforest. They are found in flooded areas at the edges of forests and probably spend a lot of time on land.

▲ *Black caiman.*

▲ *Schneider's dwarf caiman.*

► *Cuvier's dwarf caiman.*

The two dwarves

Cuvier's and Schneider's dwarf caimans are smaller than the other caimans. Their bodies are also more heavily armored, and they do not have any bony ridges or "spectacles" around their brown eyes. They have short tails and when they walk they often hold their heads high on upstretched necks, just like mammals. These differences may be because they live in more heavily forested areas than the other caimans.

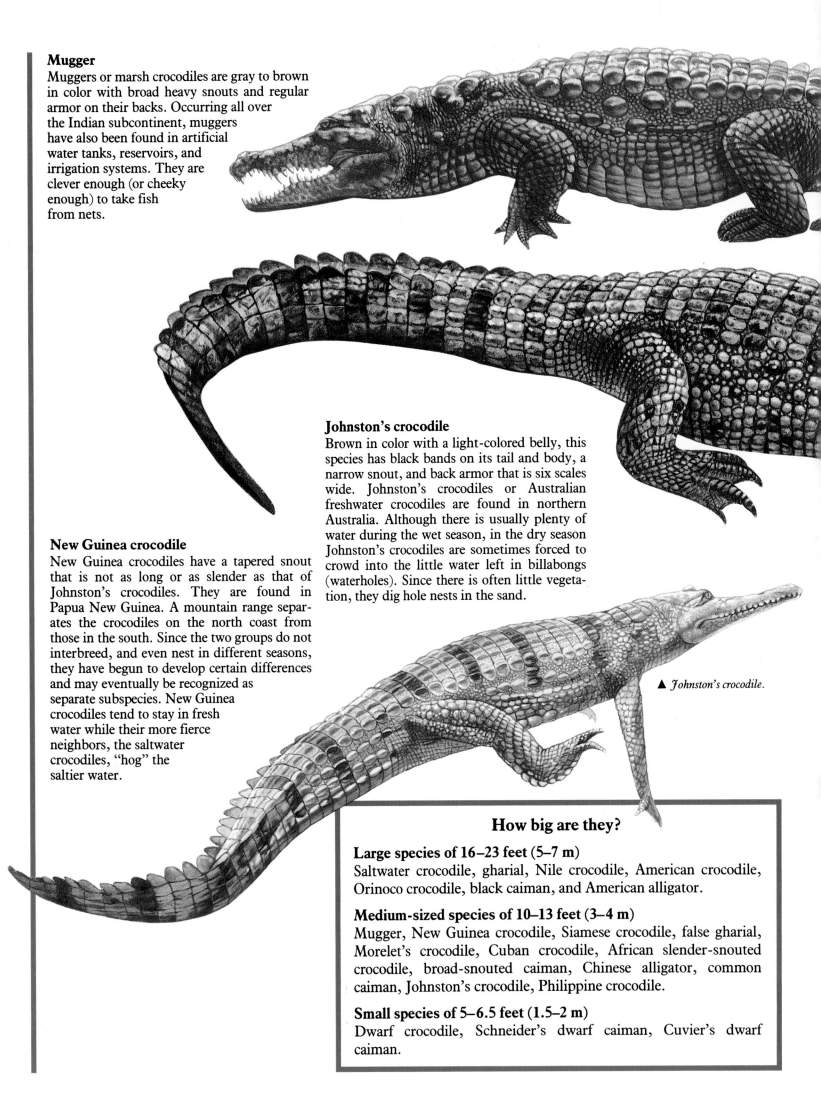

Mugger

Muggers or marsh crocodiles are gray to brown in color with broad heavy snouts and regular armor on their backs. Occurring all over the Indian subcontinent, muggers have also been found in artificial water tanks, reservoirs, and irrigation systems. They are clever enough (or cheeky enough) to take fish from nets.

Johnston's crocodile

Brown in color with a light-colored belly, this species has black bands on its tail and body, a narrow snout, and back armor that is six scales wide. Johnston's crocodiles or Australian freshwater crocodiles are found in northern Australia. Although there is usually plenty of water during the wet season, in the dry season Johnston's crocodiles are sometimes forced to crowd into the little water left in billabongs (waterholes). Since there is often little vegetation, they dig hole nests in the sand.

▲ *Johnston's crocodile.*

New Guinea crocodile

New Guinea crocodiles have a tapered snout that is not as long or as slender as that of Johnston's crocodiles. They are found in Papua New Guinea. A mountain range separates the crocodiles on the north coast from those in the south. Since the two groups do not interbreed, and even nest in different seasons, they have begun to develop certain differences and may eventually be recognized as separate subspecies. New Guinea crocodiles tend to stay in fresh water while their more fierce neighbors, the saltwater crocodiles, "hog" the saltier water.

How big are they?

Large species of 16–23 feet (5–7 m)
Saltwater crocodile, gharial, Nile crocodile, American crocodile, Orinoco crocodile, black caiman, and American alligator.

Medium-sized species of 10–13 feet (3–4 m)
Mugger, New Guinea crocodile, Siamese crocodile, false gharial, Morelet's crocodile, Cuban crocodile, African slender-snouted crocodile, broad-snouted caiman, Chinese alligator, common caiman, Johnston's crocodile, Philippine crocodile.

Small species of 5–6.5 feet (1.5–2 m)
Dwarf crocodile, Schneider's dwarf caiman, Cuvier's dwarf caiman.

▼ *Mugger.*

Siamese crocodile

Young Siamese crocodiles look quite like saltwater crocodiles and are often confused with them since they both inhabit mainland Southeast Asia and some of the Indonesian islands. But Siamese crocodiles have broader snouts and more throat scales than saltwater crocodiles. Little is known about this species, and scientists fear it may be extinct in the wild.

▲ *Siamese crocodile.*

▲ *New Guinea crocodile.*

Dwarf crocodile

What it lacks in size, the dwarf crocodile makes up for in its incredibly heavy armor, which covers the entire body, even its eyelids. Found in the tropical forests of west and central Africa, dwarf crocodiles seem to prefer slow-moving water and avoid large rivers. They are "night owls" (nocturnal) and, unlike most species, spend very little time basking in the open.

Philippine crocodile

Philippine crocodiles have broader snouts and heavier armor than any other species found in the Pacific region. Now found on only eight of the many Philippine islands, they probably once lived on all of the islands but were forced out when land on these islands was converted to rice paddies or other farms.

▲ *Dwarf crocodile.*

▲ *Philippine crocodile.*

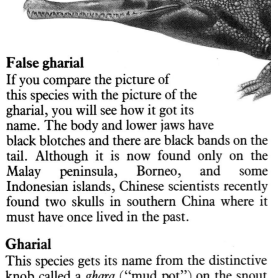

False gharial

If you compare the picture of this species with the picture of the gharial, you will see how it got its name. The body and lower jaws have black blotches and there are black bands on the tail. Although it is now found only on the Malay peninsula, Borneo, and some Indonesian islands, Chinese scientists recently found two skulls in southern China where it must have once lived in the past.

▲ *False gharial*

Gharial

This species gets its name from the distinctive knob called a *ghara* ("mud pot") on the snout of adult males. Gharials have weak legs and do not take long walks overland from one lake or river to another.

▼ *Female gharials prefer to dig their nests in steep sandy banks.*

Romulus Whitaker

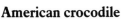

American crocodile

Adult American crocodiles have a hump in front of the eyes and their armor is irregular and uneven. They live near the coast in large rivers or lakes in southern Florida, the Caribbean, Mexico and northern South America.

▲ *American crocodile*

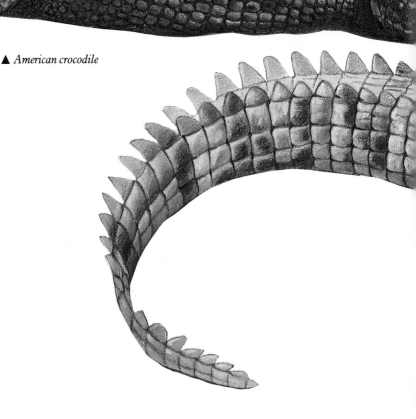

▼ *Cuban crocodile*

Cuban crocodile

Cuban crocodiles are, as their name suggests, found in Cuba where they live in the pools and channels of freshwater swamps. They have very short skulls with bumps at the back of them that look a bit like horns. Younger animals are light golden in color with black spots and bands. Adults are dark gray or black with golden yellow spots. They sometimes *interbreed* with American crocodiles, and the crossbred hatchlings often have Cuban crocodile colors but American crocodile skulls.

Did you know?

Some species of crocodiles will use their heads like sledge-hammers to knock prey into the water if they cannot get their teeth into it. One species catches fish by swimming slowly along a river bank with its tail curved toward the bank "gathering" small fish. The Nile crocodile uses its tail to bend reeds and catapult nestling birds into its ready jaws.

Morelet's crocodile

This species is darker in color, smaller, and less widespread than the American crocodile. Morelet's crocodiles have heavy neck *scales*, and there is a raised flat section running from the eyes to the snout. They are usually found in ponds, lakes, marshlands, or the upper freshwater sections of rivers, although some have recently been found in saltier river *estuaries*.

Orinoco crocodile

Orinoco crocodiles resemble American crocodiles except that they have more slender snouts and even, symmetrical armor on their backs. The two species can be confused, because both are found in the Orinoco River, although Orinoco crocodiles are usually in the freshwater upper reaches of the river, far from the coast-dwelling American crocodiles.

▲ *Orinoco crocodile*

▼ *Nile crocodile*

Nile crocodile

Nile crocodiles are dark in color with a lighter-colored belly. Although they are usually found in fresh water, some have occasionally been seen on ocean beaches in Kenya and one was seen in the sea 7 miles (11 km) off the Zululand coast. They are found throughout Africa and are notorious "man eaters."

▼ *African slender-snouted crocodile.*

African slender-snouted crocodile

A secretive crocodile found in freshwater areas of Africa's tropical forests, this species gets its name from its narrow snout. The enlarged scales on its neck are unlike the scales of other crocodiles since they are arranged in a different pattern and join the back armor. Females do not all nest at the same time, which is unusual.

Saltwater crocodile

This species is the largest — and most feared — living reptile. Saltwater crocodiles have heavy snouts with two raised ridges running from the eyes to the center of the snout. It is the most widely distributed species, and also one of the few species of crocodile often found in salt water. But beware ... despite its name, the saltwater crocodile is also found in fresh water.

▼ *Indo-Pacific saltwater crocodile*

Jean-Paul Ferrero/Auscape International

What's your address?

Did you ever write your name and address like this?

Harry Jones
309 Buena Vista Road
New Port Richey
Florida 33552
USA
Northern Hemisphere
The Earth

There may be only four people who share the same street name and number but millions share the same country and many, many millions share the Earth. In the same way there may only be a few species that share the same genus but hundreds of species share the same class and thousands share the same kingdom.

Sorting them out

Humans have always found it useful to sort and name objects, animals, and plants, as a quick way of describing them to others. The most ancient peoples probably sorted animals very simply into "good to eat," "bad to eat," "not dangerous," and "dangerous." Scientists today sort or group animals more precisely according to what they look like, features they have in common, and how they might be related to each other.

In 1758 the great Swedish naturalist Carolus Linnaeus developed a system for sorting all living things. His system is still used today. The basic unit of his system is the species. Only members of the same species can breed together and produce fertile offspring (hatchlings that are able to breed when they grow up).

Species that closely resemble each other can be grouped into a higher category called a genus (plural: genera). Each species has two scientific names — one identifies the species itself and is like your given name; the other name, like your surname, tells you what genus the species belongs to. The two names are usually Greek or Latin and are printed in *italics*. All scientists, whatever language they speak, use the same names. (The scientific names of all the species discussed in this book are given on page 67.)

A number of closely related genera can be grouped together in a subfamily. A number of subfamilies can be grouped together into a family. Families can be grouped into orders, orders into classes, classes into phyla (singular: phylum), and phyla into kingdoms.

All alligators, crocodiles, caimans, and gharials belong to the same kingdom (the animal kingdom), phylum (chordates or animals with backbones), class (reptiles), order (crocodilians), and family (crocodylidae). But they belong to three different subfamilies, eight different genera, and 22 different species (see the diagram below).

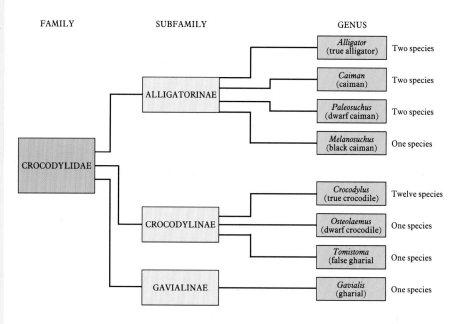

FAMILY	SUBFAMILY	GENUS	
		Alligator (true alligator)	Two species
	ALLIGATORINAE	*Caiman* (caiman)	Two species
		Paleosuchus (dwarf caiman)	Two species
CROCODYLIDAE		*Melanosuchus* (black caiman)	One species
		Crocodylus (true crocodile)	Twelve species
	CROCODYLINAE	*Osteolaemus* (dwarf crocodile)	One species
		Tomistoma (false gharial)	One species
	GAVIALINAE	*Gavialis* (gharial)	One species

▲ *Scientists now use Greek or Latin names to sort and name animal species. The American alligators shown here all share the same name, Alligator mississippiensis.*

Where do alligators and crocodiles live?

Alligators and crocodiles need both land and water to survive. In this chapter we shall look at the types of land and water (*habitats*) in which alligators live and why these habitats are in danger.

What is a habitat?

A habitat is the place where an animal lives. The habitat of any animal includes such things as the soil and water of the environment together with the plants and animals that share the habitat. All of these are linked together and depend on each other. For example, if the water in the habitat becomes polluted, plants and fish die. If they die, insects, birds, and smaller animals that feed on them also die or move elsewhere. Without insects, fish, birds, and small animals, the largest animals in the *food chain*, such as alligators and crocodiles, have nothing left to eat and they too die off or look for somewhere else to live.

Water

Most alligators and crocodiles live in the fresh water of rivers, lakes, and ponds, although saltwater crocodiles and American crocodiles appear to be able to live in saltier water. Most species prefer warm, slow-moving water where there are many water plants, but again there are exceptions. For example, the two dwarf caimans are often found in the upper reaches of rivers where the water is cooler, flows faster and has fewer plants.

There are two features of water that alligators and crocodiles can take advantage of. Water makes them buoyant (able to float), which means that swimming around in water uses less energy than walking on land. In hot climates, where most alligators and crocodiles live, the temperature of the water never gets as high as it does on land so alligators and crocodiles can avoid overheating by staying *submerged* in the cooler water.

Land

Most of the land in alligator and crocodile habitats is humid tropical forest, rainforest, or mangrove forests. The land beside lakes, rivers, and ponds is used by alligators and crocodiles for basking in the sun, which raises their body temperature when they are too cool. Some species even dig burrows on land to escape from intense cold or intense heat. But the most important function of dry land is for building nests and laying eggs. River sandbanks, lake shores, and high mounds or little islands above water are favorite nesting sites.

▶ *Pollution of the water by humans kills plants, insects, fish, birds, and eventually even larger animals like alligators and crocodiles that can find nothing left to eat in the polluted water.*

▼ *This Johnston's crocodile has adapted to the very dry conditions of its habitat in northern Australia and scoops out a nest in dry sand.*

Which countries do they live in?

Caimans live in South and Central America. Alligators are found in the south-eastern United States and in the Yangtze River of China. Crocodiles are much more widespread. They are found as far apart as northern Australia, Southeast Asia, Africa, India, Central America, South America and the Caribbean. If you live in a cooler country not mentioned in this list, you will have to travel if you want to see an alligator or crocodile in the wild.

◀ *Like all alligators and crocodiles, Nile crocodiles need land for basking and nesting as much as they need water.*

The disappearing forests

All over the world human populations are growing rapidly and there is a need for more food, more industry, more housing, and more land. Forests are being cut down to provide timber, and to clear the land for mining, farming and more homes.

This spells disaster for alligator and crocodile habitats. Cutting down the rainforests affects the land they nest on and the water around it. When trees are cut down, silt and soil are washed into the rivers and lakes making them shallower. The fish that are part of the food chain die off. Nitrates and phosphates that are usually held in the soil get washed into the water. Algae thrive on these chemicals and the oxygen level in the water gets too low for other plants and fish to survive. Without the tree roots that store water and release it slowly into the water nearby, rivers dry up more often in the dry season and flood more often in the wet season. Mine tailings, industrial and human waste pollute the water, and increased use of the river by boats disturbs the wildlife.

What can be done?

Alligators and crocodiles need help to survive. Their habitats must be protected and new habitats must be provided for them. Wildlife sanctuaries in areas of the forest protected from tree felling and planting, and new forests to replace some of those we have destroyed, can provide alligators and crocodiles with suitable new habitats.

▼ *Philippine crocodiles are extinct in the wild in some areas of the Philippines. This one is lucky to have found a new habitat in captivity.*

Michael Cermak

▼ *As well as preying on these fish, the American alligator can also help them. The alligator may provide nutrients for the plants the fish feed on and it can help to keep the waterways open so that the fish have somewhere to live.*

Did you know?

Alligators and crocodiles make a contribution to their habitats that benefits others. They feed and excrete in the water, which may help to recycle nutrients for plants on which fish feed. They open up trails and help to keep waterways open through marshlands. They deepen waterholes during droughts and provide a habitat for other animals.

Angel Alcala

Peter Parks/Oxford Scientific Films Ltd

A body built for survival

Alligators and crocodiles have more complex bodies than other reptiles. In this chapter we shall look at how their bodies are built and how they work.

▲ *These stained teeth are good for seizing prey, but no good for chewing it.*

The body

Alligators and crocodiles are long, lizard-like animals with a muscular tail for swimming. Their teeth can seize and hold prey, but they are no good for chewing. They have no lips so their mouths cannot be sealed and leak even when they are closed.

Their skin is thick and covered with scales, which shed individually rather than in large patches like other reptiles. Their armor is made up of bony buttons called osteoderms, which are embedded in the skin. They have four short legs with five partly webbed toes on the front feet and four partly webbed toes on the back feet.

Since they swallow their food unchewed, their stomachs are in two parts. A muscular "front stomach" grinds the food and the very acidic "back stomach" then digests the ground-up food. They have no bladder, and urine is passed straight out through a vent, called the *cloaca*, beneath their tails.

Seeing, hearing, and smelling

Alligators and crocodiles have eyes with a rigid, round eyeball but a vertical pupil. The vertical pupil can open wider at night to allow more light to enter. Each eye has two movable eyelids (like yours) and a transparent third eyelid that covers the eye when the animal is underwater. This third eyelid does not allow the eye to focus underwater so although alligators and crocodiles can see well — and in color — above the water, they must use senses other than sight to find prey underwater.

Alligators and crocodiles have good hearing, which is just as well since they bellow and talk to each other so much (see page 44). The outside of each ear is covered by a movable flap that stops water entering the ear canal during a dive.

Alligators and crocodiles also have a good sense of smell. Experiments in captivity show that even young alligators can pick up smells in the air.

▲ *Alligators and crocodiles only have four toes, joined by webbing, on their back feet.*

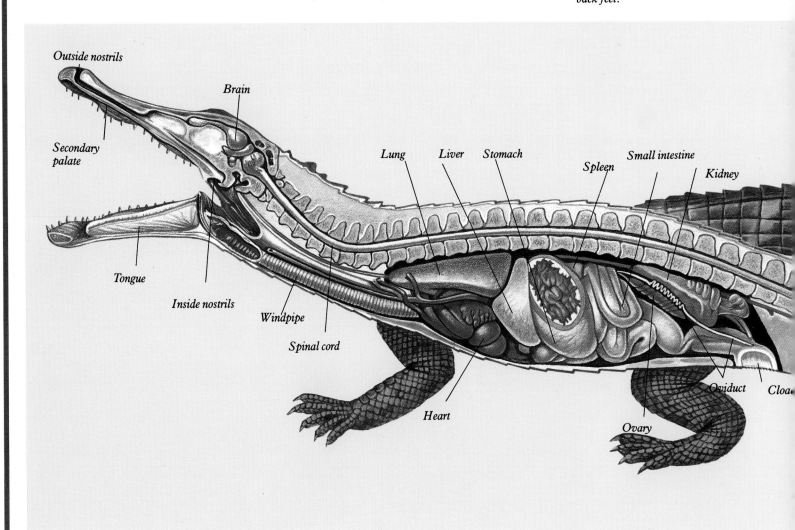

Outside nostrils

Brain

Secondary palate

Tongue

Inside nostrils

Windpipe

Spinal cord

Lung

Liver

Stomach

Spleen

Small intestine

Kidney

Heart

Ovary

Oviduct

Cloaca

C. Pollitt/Australasian Nature Transparencies

David P. Maitland/Seaphot Limited: Planet Earth Pictures/Transglobe Agency

▲ ▶ *In the dark the pupil of the eye becomes wide open and round to catch more light (above). In bright sunlight the pupil becomes narrow and vertical to cut down the glare (right).*

▼ *Alligator and crocodile insides are a bit "mixed up". Some of their organs are like those of other reptiles, but some are more like mammal organs.*

Did you know?

Crocodiles absorb salt through their skins, and when they eat and drink. Saltwater turtles lose salt through what were once tear *glands*. The marine iguana breathes a salty spray out through its nose. Crocodiles have salt glands in their tongues. Scientists can understand why saltwater crocodiles have these glands but it is a mystery why other crocodiles that never lived near salt water also have these glands.

Laurence Taplin

Scales

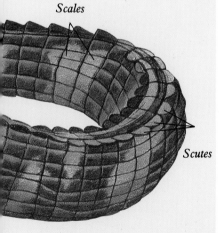

Scutes

Frieder Sauer/Bruce Coleman Ltd

▲ *This Cuban crocodile may be watching, smelling, or listening to something. It can do all of these very well.*

Breathing

Alligators and crocodiles can breathe underwater even when their mouths are open, as long as the nostrils on the tip of the snout are above the water. Nasal passages run from these nostrils above the secondary palate (made up of three bones) straight into the throat. A valve formed by a fleshy fold at the back of the palate meets a similar fold in the tongue, and this keeps water out of the throat. Alligators and crocodiles have lungs made up of many small spongy chambers that trap air. They also have a sort of diaphragm to give extra help in breathing.

Around and around goes the blood

Alligators and crocodiles are the only reptiles to have a mammal-type heart that is divided into four chambers. This allows oxygen-carrying blood to be separated from blood that no longer carries oxygen. Mammals, alligators, and crocodiles can control the flow of blood, oxygen, and heat to various parts of the body in two ways: the heart rate can speed up or slow down, or the blood vessels can widen or

narrow. For example, if an alligator or crocodile gets too hot, the blood vessels widen, blood flows to the surface of the skin and the extra heat is lost in the water. During a dive, however, the heart rate slows down, and although the blood vessels become narrower to reduce blood flowing to the muscles, oxygen in the blood can still reach vital organs like the heart and brain.

▼ *The two species of alligator live in areas where winters can be very cold. They are able to survive in temperatures that would not suit other species.*

Lynn M. Stone/Bruce Coleman Ltd

Raymond A. Mendez/Animals Animals

▲ *The nostrils at the very end of alligator and crocodile snouts are often the only part of the animal that can be seen above the water.*

Peter Jackson/Bruce Coleman Ltd

Keeping a constant temperature

Alligators and crocodiles are poikilothermic; that is, their body temperature rises or falls according to the temperature outside.

If you are too cold you move close to a heater and if you are too hot you move somewhere cooler. Alligators and crocodiles also behave in certain ways to keep their bodies at a comfortable temperature. To keep cool they stay underwater in the heat of the day. To keep warm they bask in the sun on land or stay in the water at night since it cools more slowly than land.

Alligator and crocodile bodies are designed so carefully that they have been able to survive for millions of years with very few changes.

▲ *These gharials move in and out of the water in order to keep their bodies at a constant temperature.*

▶ *The large, pink, fleshy fold at the back of this American alligator's mouth stops water entering the breathing passages when it is underwater. By opening its mouth above the water the alligator allows water to evaporate into the air and cools itself down.*

Robert C. Simpson/Tom Stack & Associates

▼ *This saltwater crocodile's body is perfectly suited to its lifestyle.*

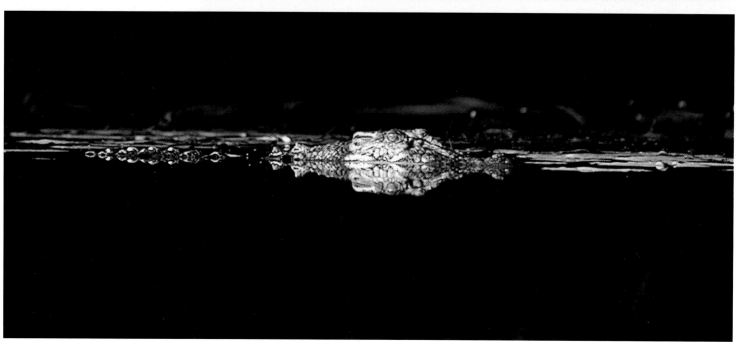

Jean-Paul Ferrero/Auscape International

Getting around

Swimming

Alligators and crocodiles are excellent swimmers, even underwater. They hold their legs close to their bodies so that they are more streamlined and drag (resistance to the water) is reduced. They usually cruise slowly in the water with gentle S-shaped sweeps of their powerful tails. However, when they are chasing something — or being chased — they swim very rapidly and even leap out of the water in a dolphin-like tail walk.

When they are floating in water they hold their legs out to the side to help them to balance.

▲ *With slow sweeps of its powerful tail, this saltwater crocodile swims smoothly through the water, using very little energy.*

Walking, galloping, and crawling

Alligators and crocodiles basking on land do not move around much. But sometimes they do need to move around on land to escape from danger or to find new water or shelter from heat and cold. Although they are not nearly as graceful on land as they are in water they can move quite well when they want to. They have three different ways of moving on land.

If they are in no special hurry, they use a high walk. Unlike other reptiles, alligators and crocodiles can hold their legs almost upright beneath their bodies so that the belly and tail are raised off the ground. At a stately 0.2–0.3 miles (0.3–0.5 km) an hour, they walk just like other four-legged mammals. They can increase the speed into a trot but if they move too fast they lose their balance and crash to the ground!

Smaller crocodiles can even gallop. The back legs push the crocodile forward in a leap. The body straightens and the front legs move forward to catch the body at the end of the leap. The back legs then swing forward again for the next leap. With this bounding gallop, small crocodiles can reach speeds of up to 10 miles (17 km) an hour. This is not very fast

Joanna Van Gruisen/Ardea London

Best leg forward

Alligators and crocodiles use the same sequence of leg movements that other four-legged animals use when walking — watch your cat or dog closely the next time it walks. The front right leg goes forward first, then the back left leg. The front left leg goes forward next and finally the right back leg. This well-balanced, diagonal sequence is then repeated.

compared with some mammals — but it is fast enough to surprise a possible victim.

The belly crawl is less graceful but very effective if an alligator or crocodile is startled or wants to slip quietly into the water. On its belly with its legs splayed out to the side, the alligator or crocodile twists its body from side to side and "rows" with its legs. In this way it thrashes and slides on its belly to slither quietly into the water.

▼ *Leaping out of the water, possibly to catch a passing bird or a fish thrown from a boat, this saltwater crocodile seems to be "walking" on its tail.*

◄ ▲ *To get around on land, alligators and crocodiles walk, crawl (left), or even gallop (above).*

Bill Green

J.M. La-Roque/Auscape International

What do alligators and crocodiles eat?

Alligators and crocodiles eat insects, frogs, spiders, shellfish, snails, birds, fish, other reptiles, and mammals. But how much of each type of food they eat depends on their size, species, and where they live.

Differences in diet
Baby hatchlings of most species eat mainly insects, but as they get slightly bigger they move on to tadpoles, snails, crabs, shrimps, and small fish. As they grow even larger they eat more, and larger, fish. They also begin to eat birds, reptiles, and mammals — small and large. Not only are adult appetites and stomachs larger but their snouts are stronger so that they are able to catch prey that would escape from a smaller alligator or crocodile.

The food that an alligator or crocodile eats also depends on its habitat. Alligators and crocodiles living in the salty waters of lagoons and estuaries eat different food than their cousins who live in fresh water because the type of food around them is different.

The shape of the snout is also important in determining diet. Long, slender snouts are ideally suited to catching fish since they can sweep through the water and snap sideways to grab a fish faster and more easily than a heavy, round snout. The gharial and crocodiles with narrow snouts eat a lot of fish. They also eat other food, because they are agile and can catch bats or birds by leaping into the air. Alligators and crocodiles with heavy, broad snouts eat larger prey, especially mammals, because their snouts are strong enough to overpower a bigger victim.

Obviously the type of mammals they eat depends on the wildlife available in the country they live.

How do alligators and crocodiles catch their food?
Alligators and crocodiles are patient but lazy hunters. They do not scour the countryside searching for food and using up vital energy. Instead, they lie hidden in the water waiting for a meal to come to them. They are not fussy eaters — if it can be eaten and caught without much effort, any prey will do. Alligators and crocodiles also remember where they have caught food successfully in the past and will patiently sit and wait at the same place for the next meal to come along.

Alligators and crocodiles use three different techniques for catching food — lunging, sweeping, and leaping.

▲ *A Nile crocodile grabs a warthog by the nearest part of its body, in this case the scruff of the neck.*

▼ *Pelicans are heavy birds and slow to get airborne — too slow for this lunging Nile crocodile.*

How often do they eat?
Many alligators and crocodiles are found with empty stomachs. Scientists believe that hatchlings can survive for up to four months without eating and adults may last for up to two years between meals. Most alligators and crocodiles eat only 50 full meals a year (compared with your 1,000). They also eat very little during winter when they are sluggish and inactive.

◄ *A hatchling meets its next meal. The smallest hatchlings will eat only insects for every meal.*

From a submerged position in the water, an alligator or crocodile will make a lunge at an animal, alone or in a group, on the river bank or in the water. In a quick burst of energy it will grab the nearest part of its victim, often the muzzle that is dipping into the water for a drink. It then pulls its victim into deeper water and holds the muzzle under the water, or spins the animal in a "death roll" (around and around) to drown it.

Some species are very skilled at sweeping the water for fish. When a fish comes near enough it is grabbed in a sideways snap and pinned down in the shallows to prevent it escaping, or even held down on land until it stops struggling. Then it is eaten.

Alligators and crocodiles can leap up to 5 feet (1.5 m) out of the water to snap at hovering insects, birds, or bats that are flying too low for their own good, or at mammals climbing trees.

Sharing food

When shoals of fish approach a narrow channel, Nile crocodiles spread out in a line and snap at the fish that come their way. They never move out of line to leave an escape route for the fish, and they do not fight over the food. When a large mammal, too tough and too large for one crocodile to manage alone is caught, others will gather to share the feast. Forming a circle around the carcass, each crocodile waits its turn, moves in to grab a chunk of flesh then retreats to the outer edge of the circle to eat its fill and patiently wait for the next bite.

Alligators and crocodiles are skilled, efficient hunters. They catch food by using stealth, surprise, and as little effort as possible.

Jonathan Scott/Planet Earth Pictures

▲ *This zebra was possibly having a quiet drink when one of these crocodiles grabbed its sensitive muzzle. Too big for one crocodile to eat alone, the zebra meal is shared with hungry friends.*

Jonathan Scott/Planet Earth Pictures

▶ *Do these wildebeeste crossing an African river see the stealthy crocodile submerged in the water, choosing its dinner?*

Walking to its own death
The muzzles of many animals are very sensitive when grabbed by sharp alligator or crocodile teeth. To avoid further pain in its muzzle, a victim will often walk into the water without resisting. The alligator or crocodile then gets a meal without too much of a struggle and its victim has more than a sore muzzle to complain about.

Swallowing and digesting

What big teeth you have!

Alligators and crocodiles have an impressive mouthful of teeth. The sharp teeth (called canines) puncture and grip prey. The blunt molars are used for crushing prey. But none of the teeth have strong roots so they come out easily and cannot be used for chewing. Alligator and crocodile jaws cannot move sideways for chewing either. They have to swallow their food whole or break it into smaller pieces that they can then swallow.

How do they swallow?

With a firm grip on its food, an alligator or crocodile lifts its head above water and maneuvers the food into the right position. It then tosses its head back so that the food falls down its throat. Most fish are just the right size and shape to be swallowed whole, but they are swallowed head first so that the sharp spines on their backs do not injure the alligator or crocodile's throat or gullet.

If a fish or mammal is too large to swallow whole, the alligator or crocodile grips the food with the unwanted pieces outside its mouth and shakes its head vigorously so that the unwanted heads or legs are shaken off. If the food is very large the alligator or crocodile often spins and rolls over repeatedly with a firm grip on the piece of flesh it wants until eventually the piece is torn away from the body. Sometimes this does not work and a second alligator or crocodile may hold the carcass still while the first alligator or crocodile rolls; or both may grip the carcass and roll in opposite directions to tear the food apart.

Gary Retherford/Bruce Coleman Ltd

Jeff Foot/Survival Anglia Ltd

▲ Whenever an alligator or crocodile loses a tooth, another tooth is always waiting underneath to fill the gap. A crocodile with no teeth would starve to death.

◄ Fish are the ideal shape for swallowing whole. If swallowed head first, the spines that grow in the direction of the tail will not scratch the American alligator's gullet.

◄ This saltwater crocodile does not need to chew the curlew it has just taken. It will swallow the bird whole or shake its head violently to break off the bird's legs.

David McGonigal/Photobank

Michael Cermak

Losing teeth

Human beings have only two sets of teeth — baby (or first) teeth and second teeth. If the second teeth fall out, then false teeth are the only answer. Alligators and crocodiles are lucky. They go on and on replacing their teeth. A replacement tooth grows beneath each existing tooth. When the old tooth eventually comes out, the new tooth is already waiting to take its place.

Digesting

Alligators and crocodiles sometimes swallow hard objects such as stones, which are rubbed together by the muscular gizzard and help break up food. Alligators and crocodiles also have higher levels of acid in their stomachs than other vertebrates. This acid helps them to break down and consume every part of the food they eat — including the bones.

You use food to provide you with energy and help you grow. Alligators and crocodiles store most of the energy in their food as fat on various parts of the body, especially the back and tail, in case they have to wait a long time until the next meal. As a result they do not have much spare energy for moving about, they get tired very quickly, and they do not grow very fast.

► Alligators and crocodiles juggle their food into the right position before tossing their heads back so that the food falls down the throat.

T. Pooley

Birth and baby care

Alligators and crocodiles mate in the water but lay their eggs in nests that are built or dug on land. In this chapter we shall look at how the young are born and looked after by their parents.

Male sex organs
Males usually grow faster and larger than females. They have a bent penis that is usually hidden inside the body. Muscles and tissue in the cloaca force the penis out during mating. Sperm is not carried inside the penis but passes along a single open groove on the top of the penis.

Female sex organs
When the female releases an ovum (egg cell) it passes from the ovary into a twisted, spiraling passage called an oviduct where it is fertilized by the male sperm. As it spirals its way down the oviduct, eggshell surrounds the ovum. The completed eggs than pass out through the cloaca into the nest.

Nesting
Some time after mating all the females begin to make their nests.

Alligators, caimans, and some crocodiles build mound nests out of fresh vegetation, soil, and leaves. The female scratches the soil and vegetation into a pile and uses her body to press it into a firm mound. She then prepares an egg chamber by scooping out a hole in the mound with her back feet. The decomposing vegetation keeps the nest and eggs warm.

Other crocodiles and the gharial dig hole nests in the sand by scraping sand backwards with their hind feet. Some species dig trial nests possibly to check that the temperature is right for *incubating* (hatching) the eggs before they dig their real nests. The warmth of the sand below and over the top of the eggs keeps the eggs warm.

Egg laying
In the right position over her nest, the female begins to lay her eggs — one every half minute or so. The number of eggs in one clutch varies from 15 eggs to 80 eggs depending on the age and species of the female. While she is laying her eggs the female is usually quite tame and researchers have even been able to catch the eggs as they are being laid.

Guarding and opening the nest
Female alligators and crocodiles guard their nests fiercely and will attack any animals or humans that come too close. They often eat no food during the 70–90 days that it takes for the eggs to incubate.

When the eggs are ready to hatch, the hatchlings start making yelps, croaks, or grunts. The female then digs up the eggs by scratching away any covering and using her

Using her back feet the female mugger scrapes away the sand to form a hole nest (above). She then lays 25-35 eggs (top right) and scrapes sand over them to keep them warm. Until the eggs hatch she will stay near the eggs and defend them fiercely (bottom).

Ernest Neal/Seaphot Limited/Planet Earth Pictures

▲ *These hatchling Nile crocodiles stick very close together after they are born. Although you cannot see her, the mother will certainly be close by.*

▼ *This hatchling has started to break out of its egg, but some of its brothers and sisters being born at the same time may need the mother's help to crack their eggs open.*

teeth to bite through roots that have grown around the eggs. She will help to crack any unopened eggs by rolling them gently between her tongue and the roof of her mouth. She carries the new hatchlings in her mouth down to the water where she gently releases them.

Boy or girl?

The embryo (fetus) within a newly laid egg is neither male or female. The temperature at which the egg is incubated during the first few weeks in the nest determines whether the hatchling will be male or female. For crocodile hatchlings, high incubation temperatures produce all females; medium temperatures produce all males; and low temperatures produce all females. For alligator and caiman hatchlings, high temperatures produce all males; medium temperatures produce a mixture of males and females; and low temperatures produce all females.

Looking after the hatchlings

Hatchlings stay close together in a group near their mothers for some time after they are born. They often use their mother's head and back as a basking platform. If they stray too far from the group, they will yelp for help and the mother, or any other adult nearby, will rescue them and carry them back to the group.

It seems a shame that despite all the mother's effort and care, many alligator and crocodile eggs and hatchlings die. Many nests are flooded before the eggs hatch, and the hatchlings are easy prey for birds, fish, and even other crocodiles and alligators.

Anthony Bannister/NHPA

The breeding season

The time of year that each species breeds seems to depend on local rainfall. Some species breed during the dry season, and others breed in the wet season. Because alligators and crocodiles are widespread throughout the world, there is probably one species breeding every month of the year. Some species breed in the same place that they spend the non-breeding months. Other species make long journeys to special breeding beaches.

▲ *This American alligator may look fierce to us but to the hatchling basking on her head she is a caring and protective mother.*

Choosing a mate

When the breeding season approaches, adult alligators and crocodiles gather in large groups. The larger males establish their mating territories. Females are allowed into these territories, but other males are frightened off by body signals such as raised heads and tails or jaws slapped on the water. The jaw-slaps (see pages 44-45) may also attract females.

Females often start the *courting* but either sex may follow or circle a possible mate until the right moment or partner comes along. During courting alligators and crocodiles touch each other a lot, especially around the sensitive head and neck. The male may rub the underside of his throat across the female's head and neck. This rubbing releases a scent from the glands under his chin. He may also submerge beside the female and blow bubbles from his nostrils or throat — obviously females find bubbles romantic! The two often rub snouts and may also push each other under the water, possibly to see how big and strong their partner is.

The female will show that she has accepted the male by lifting her head or by submerging under the water. Sometimes she opens her mouth and makes a long, throaty growl. Some species, like American alligators, are very noisy during courting and both partners bellow constantly — and can be heard for some distance. Other species, especially in wide open habitats, rely on being seen rather than heard and are silent during courting.

Courting is a long, slow process that may last for a number of hours before the male and female mate. Sometimes the courting is not successful and the two will drift apart to find another possible mate.

Alligators and crocodiles are polygamous, that is, males have more than one "wife." Males may court and mate with one female for a number of days before moving on to another female, or court and mate with a number of females, one after the other.

In the world of alligators and crocodiles, big is beautiful, at least among males. The larger the male the more likely he is to be able to defend his mating territory and to attract a number of females on to his territory.

Male alligators and crocodiles may not be very faithful mates but they often turn out to be good fathers. They will help the female to guard the nest and hatchlings. Sometimes they also help her to open the nest and carry the young to the water.

Jeffrey W. Lang

▲ *A male and female New Guinea crocodile meet and form a couple.*

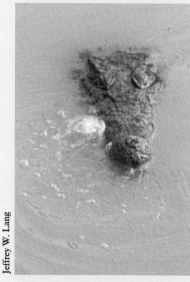

Jeffrey W. Lang

▲ *The female submerges and blows bubbles beside the male to impress him.*

Jeffrey W. Lang

▲ *The female raises her snout to show that she has accepted the male and they mate in the water.*

▼ *They may look like a courting couple, but these two Nile crocodiles are both male, and they are actually fighting over mating territory.*

Adrian Warren/Ardea London

David Hughes/Bruce Coleman Ltd

◄ *The smaller female American alligator tries to push the male under the water to see if he is big and strong enough to make a good mate.*

Early death

Alligators and crocodiles are most likely to die while they are still in their eggs or during their first year of life. They die from natural causes such as floods or are killed and eaten by predators.

▲ *Heavy rain can flood alligator and crocodile nests, destroying all the eggs inside them. The mother cannot lay another clutch of eggs until after the next year's breeding season.*

Death in the nest

Many alligator and crocodile eggs die before they hatch. Female alligators and crocodiles lay a large number of eggs, but they lay only one clutch a year (unlike most species of birds that may produce two or three smaller broods each year). If something happens to their eggs, alligators and crocodiles cannot lay another clutch of eggs to make up for the ones they have lost.

Birds sit on top of their eggs and can therefore control the temperature and dampness in their nests. Alligators and crocodiles lay their eggs in a nest in the ground, and although they stay near the nest they do not sit on top of it. The eggs inside the nest have little protection against the weather.

Alligator and crocodile eggs are porous (full of pores or tiny holes) to allow oxygen to reach the growing babies inside. But during heavy rains, water can also get into the eggs and drown the embryos. Heavy rain can also make the nest too cool for the eggs to incubate. Too little rain can be just as bad. In a hot drought the eggs overheat and dry out and some or all of the eggs will perish.

Alligators and crocodiles build their nests on land near water. The female carefully chooses a site for her nest that is above the usual high-water level, but during tropical storms this land, and the nests on it, can flood and the embryos can drown. Even if the nests escape flooding, they may become very damp, which can cause fungus to grow on some eggs. The eggs with the fungus will die, but harmful gases given off by the "bad" egg can also destroy the other healthy eggs packed tightly around it.

Weather conditions are not the only danger facing the eggs. Eggs with very thin shells, or even with no shell at all, are occasionally laid; these rarely survive. Sometimes eggs laid by one female are accidentally dug up and destroyed by another female digging a nest in the same place. A careless mother may pierce some of her own eggs with her sharp claws or she may squash them.

▶ *This Nile crocodile is one of the lucky ones and has survived to become an adult. But there are still dangers to face. In a fight the bigger and heavier hippopotamus would probably win.*

Death by fire

In Botswana in Africa farmers burn off reeds and papyrus to provide grazing for their livestock. Unfortunately the burning is usually done during the crocodiles' nesting season. Nests and eggs are burnt and destroyed. Occasionally adults also fail to escape in time and are burnt to death.

Did you know?

Researchers are studying the development of alligator babies by removing the top one-third of the eggshell. While the baby continues to grow normally, they can watch and photograph its development. They can see what causes abnormalities such as cleft palates and even use microsurgery to repair the damage before the alligator is born. This knowledge is very useful for similar problems in human fetuses.

Anthony Bannister/NHPA

Richard Matthews/Seaphot Limited/Planet Earth Pictures

Beware the hungry giant lizard

No crocodile's nest is safe from the hungry, prowling monitor lizard. This giant lizard is found in Africa, Asia, and Australia where many crocodiles are also found. In some places monitor lizards may be responsible for stealing more than half of all the crocodile eggs laid each year.

Death of hatchlings

If the mother fails to return to release the hatchlings at birth they may die since they often need help to crack open their eggs and dig themselves out of the nest.

If the incubation temperature in the nest has been too high or too low, or if the mother is very young or very old, some of the hatchlings will be born with defects such as spina bifida (where the covering of the vertebrae is incomplete), blindness or cleft palate (a split or hole in the roof of the mouth). The chances of these hatchlings surviving are very low. It is difficult enough for a strong, healthy hatchling to avoid being taken by predators, but a weak or abnormal hatchling is an even easier target.

No longer a baby

As they grow larger, alligators and crocodiles have less to fear. There are only a few predators large enough (and brave enough!) to take on a fully grown alligator or crocodile. Humans are among the few predators still to be feared since they kill adult alligators and crocodiles out of fear, for their skins, or just for sport. Other alligators and crocodiles can also pose a threat since death in combat or by cannibalism (eating another of your species) can sometimes occur.

Alligators and crocodiles have less chance than you do of being born safely and living to a ripe old age because of the dangers they face in the wild.

T. Pooley

41

Deadly enemies

There are many predators that prey on alligators and crocodiles. The smaller and more vulnerable the alligator or crocodile, the higher is the chance of being killed by a predator.

Alligator and crocodile eggs are considered a delicacy by many predators. Hatchlings also make a tasty meal; and adults, although less appetizing, sometimes meet a predator that will try to make a meal of them.

The list of possible predators includes leopards, bears, wild pigs, dogs, foxes, raccoons, opossums, skunks, mongooses, coatis (closely related to the raccoon), monkeys, baboons, rats, giant lizards, snakes, many species of birds, turtles, and fish. Quite a frightening list!

Predators vary from country to country. American alligator eggs and hatchlings will not be taken by leopards, baboons or a giant lizard since these are not found in the United States. But the mother alligator will always be on the look out for raccoons, opossums, skunks, black bears, and birds of prey.

Some predators such as lions, hippopotamuses, and elephants will kill Nile crocodiles in Africa. Anacondas (giant snakes that crush their victims to death) prey on medium-sized caimans in Central and South America. Leopards and tigers in Asia are not afraid to try to make a meal of an adult crocodile.

It makes the dangers in our lives, such as speeding cars, seem small in comparison!

Martin Wendler/NHPA

Q. How can an ant kill a crocodile?

A. On the shores of Lake St. Lucia in Zululand, cocktail ants destroy crocodile eggs, unborn babies, and even hatchlings. They follow the scent trail of a "bad" egg and tunnel beneath the surface to get to the nest. They can nibble their way into all the eggs and kill the growing babies while the unsuspecting mother watches out for larger predators above ground.

T. Pooley

A.J. Deane/Bruce Coleman Ltd

▲ *These marabou storks near Lake Kenya use their bills to probe the sand for crocodile nests and eggs. But they keep well away from the mother crocodile.*

▲ *The anaconda of South America can grow larger than a caiman and is perfectly capable of killing one, although this does not happen regularly.*

Harlingue-Viollet/H. Roger Viollet

▲ *This Nile crocodile was caught and killed at Lake Victoria in Central Africa.*

Q. Who is the worst predator of them all?

A. Humans destroy more alligators and crocodiles than any other predator does. In many parts of the world alligator and crocodile eggs are collected for food or medicine. Nesting females are often killed and their nests destroyed by hunters. Alligators and crocodiles of any size are shot for their skins or because they are thought to be dangerous.

Michael Freeman/Bruce Coleman Ltd

◄ *The coati of South America is related to the American raccoon. It uses its claws to open caiman nests and scoop out the eggs (for breakfast!).*

Getting along together

Many people think of alligators and crocodiles as solitary predators lurking in ambush in the water. In fact, alligators and crocodiles have a remarkable social life quite unlike that of other reptiles.

Passing on messages

Alligators and crocodiles pass messages to each other with sounds, body language, smells, and touch. From an early age hatchlings learn to understand these signals, just as you learnt to understand human signals (like a smile or "goo goo") as a baby.

Alligators and crocodiles use these signals in daily life, when they are gathered together in a group (in the wild or in captivity), and when they are courting, or fighting, during the breeding season.

Sounds

Alligators and crocodiles use their vocal cords to "talk" to each other (see page 46). They can also make other sounds that do not use their vocal cords, just as you do when you clap or whistle.

One of the most common sounds made by most species is the jawslap or headslap. The alligator or crocodile lifts its head out of the water then closes its jaws as if biting the surface of the water. The sound is like the noise of a flat shovel being slapped on the top of the water.

Another sound is made by the alligator or crocodile rapidly squeezing its trunk muscles just beneath the surface of the water. The vibrations travel quickly over long distances underwater, and although you would not be able to hear them, another alligator or crocodile could.

Many species also make sounds by breathing out through their throats or nostrils. These sounds vary from soft, purring or cough-like noises and low guttural sounds (like clearing your throat), to hisses from the nostrils.

Jeffrey W. Lang

◄ *The American crocodile uses a jawslap to warn other crocodiles that they should not stray into his territory.*

Jeffrey W. Lang

◄ *Although we can see the ripples and bubbles around this American alligator as it squeezes its trunk muscles, we cannot hear the vibrations that are easily heard by other crocodiles.*

▼ *Morelet's crocodile*

▼ *This large group of New Guinea crocodiles constantly pass messages to each other that they can understand.*

Jeffrey W. Lang

Body language

Alligators and crocodiles signal their intentions to others by body postures and movements.

Lifting the head, back, and tail out of the water or thrashing the water with the tail usually means "watch out! I am the best, the biggest or the strongest!" Large animals use these signals to frighten away others. In this way they can win the best mates or the best basking sites.

When a bigger, meaner alligator or crocodile approaches, a weaker, smaller animal will submerge itself in the water leaving only its head above the water. It will open its jaws, and hold its head still for a moment. A smaller animal that does not make these signals, which show he or she does not want to fight, may be grabbed and bitten by the bigger animal.

Group behavior

Hatchlings usually remain in a crèche or nursery group near their nest sites. Often a parent stays with the group to protect them but even when there is no adult present, hatchlings will stick together in a group. This probably helps them to stay alive. A single hatchling is no match for most predators but a large group will make noisy distress calls when danger approaches and adults will rush to their rescue.

As they get older, alligators and crocodiles do not usually stay in such tightly knit groups. They will, however, gather in a loose group on certain occasions such as when basking, nesting, or sharing food. When water is scarce during a long dry spell, alligators and crocodiles of all ages seem to share what little water is available and forget — for the time being — about protecting their own territory or competing for who is biggest and strongest.

Slap, bubble, and bellow

Some species use the jawslap alone to pass on messages. But other species follow the jawslap by submerging in the water and blowing bubbles through their nostrils. Noisy species roar or bellow after jawslapping while others thrash their tails in the water. Jawslapping is "infectious", when one alligator or crocodile jawslaps, others nearby immediately jawslap back.

▲ *By submerging her body in the water and lifting her head, this female American crocodile tells the passing male that she does not want to fight.*

The "loudmouths" of the reptile world

Alligators and crocodiles start making sounds while still in their eggs and continue to use their voices as they get older.

Hatchlings of all species yelp and grunt constantly, especially when faced with danger, a new situation, or when feeding. Other hatchlings and adults can tell the difference between a distress call, a feeding call, and a greeting.

The noisy species

As they get older some species get even noisier! The roars and bellows of the noisiest species, the American alligator, can be heard up to 165 yards (160 m) away and are as loud as the noise made by a small aircraft propeller. When one alligator starts bellowing the others join in, and these bellowing choruses can last up to half an hour usually in the early mornings or late afternoons during the breeding season.

Even scientists can identify individual alligators by the bellow they make, so keeping track of friends and possible mates (of the opposite sex) must be fairly easy for the alligators.

Alligators can, however, "talk" softly as well. Males and females make quiet cough-like purrs when they are courting. A low growl is less friendly and usually warns of a fight to come. Adults grunt in reply to calls from smaller alligators and hiss when an intruder approaches.

Mike Price/Bruce Coleman Ltd

Ready when you are!

In a laboratory experiment a microphone was buried with alligator eggs. Tapping sounds from inside one egg were answered within a few seconds by similar sounds from the other eggs. Since the hatchlings are all born at the same time, perhaps the eggs are telling each other and their mother that now is the time to hatch.

▲ Hatchlings yelp and grunt to each other and their mothers when they are hungry, frightened, or just saying "Hello".

Reg Morrison/Auscape International

◄ A female saltwater crocodile produces a throaty repetitive roar when approached by another adult crocodile.

Chinese alligators have explosive roars but are not as noisy as their American cousins. Common caimans are almost as noisy as American alligators, while among the crocodiles the Siamese crocodile wins first prize as the noisiest. African slender-snouted crocodiles have a roar that sounds like a truck backfiring. Nile crocodiles, New Guinea crocodiles, and muggers give a throaty roar to warn off other crocodiles.

The silent species

Some species of crocodiles and the gharial rarely use their voices, although they too have vocal cords and can presumably use them when it is necessary.

Species living in open habitats use their voices less often. Since they can be easily seen by others, they do not need to make their presence known by bellowing or roaring.

▼ *Muggers are not as "talkative" as some species, but they sometimes roar to frighten others away.*

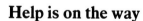

Help is on the way

When staff at a crocodile farm in Papua New Guinea picked up a stray hatchling, it called loudly. Immediately all the adults lying quietly in the pond became frantic. They swam toward the yelping hatchling making deep calls and jawslaps. The largest male even charged the fence where staff were holding the hatchling. It must be nice to know that everyone will rally round when you need help.

◀ *Caimans are almost as noisy as American alligators and if a hatchling were to yelp in distress this lazy looking group would soon be heard answering back.*

Attack!

Alligators and crocodiles are feared as vicious "man eaters" but most species are not dangerous to humans. In this chapter we shall look at the few species that do attack humans, and why and how they attack.

"Man eaters"

The Nile crocodile of Africa and the saltwater crocodile of Southeast Asia and northern Australia are the only species that deserve their fearsome reputation. These large and aggressive crocodiles are responsible for most crocodile attacks on humans.

Five other species (American crocodiles, Orinoco crocodiles, American alligators, muggers and black caimans) are known to attack humans on rare occasions. The remaining fifteen species almost never attack humans.

Why do they attack?

One reason for an attack is hunger. When alligators and crocodiles are hungry they will take whatever food is readily available — a human adult or child at the edge of the water may be the closest victim.

Large male alligators and crocodiles defend their territories and will attack any intruder, including people, wandering into their territory. Both males and females also defend nests and hatchlings, and will attack anything that comes too close to the nest.

Human beings themselves are often partly to blame for alligator and crocodile attacks. They know that they are in danger in the water but still people enter water where they know alligators and crocodiles are found.

How does an alligator or crocodile attack?

An alligator or crocodile that is about to attack will submerge under water with only its eyes and nostrils above the water. It lies in wait without moving or making a sound until a victim — human or animal — comes along.

Most victims are totally unaware that the animal is there until it attacks. The victim is often ankle-deep or knee-deep in the water when the alligator or crocodile makes a lunge and grabs hold of the nearest part of the body.

▲ *Despite the warning notice, these people are cooling off in water where the saltwater crocodile is known to live.*

> ### Killers or scavengers?
> Human artifacts, such as bracelets and rings, were often found in the stomachs of dead gharials in India. Many scientists now believe that these artifacts came from the dead bodies cremated or floated down the rivers on rafts according to Indian burial practices. The gharials in the river swallowed the hard objects to help them digest their food.

▲ *Gharial*

Mirror Australian Telegraphic Publications

It then drags the victim into deeper water to either drown him or her or kill the victim with bone-crushing bites.

Since alligators and crocodiles cannot chew they have to break the body into smaller pieces that can be swallowed whole. The body is held above the water and thrashed to pieces with violent shakes. Heads, arms, legs, and clothing may be strewn around in the process.

Nile crocodile attacks in Africa

Africa has many dangerous animals — lions, leopards, hippopotamuses, rhinoceroses, and elephants. But the Nile crocodile is the most abundant and the most dangerous of all to humans.

Adult Nile crocodiles are very aggressive and can grow to 21 feet (6.5 m) in length and 2,200 pounds (1,000 kg) in weight — much larger than any human being. They are found in rivers, streams, swamps, lagoons, lakes, and floodplains over most of Africa. There are also millions of tribal peoples who water livestock, bathe, wash clothes, fish, and use small canoes in the same waters. To these people, crocodiles are a natural hazard that they face daily.

Many villages are isolated and without telephones or radio, so many attacks are not reported. But of the attacks that have been reported, most occurred during the breeding season when the crocodiles were most active and had started feeding again after the winter.

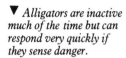

▶ *These women of the Tembe-Thonga tribe know that Nile crocodiles are in the water, but their families must eat and so they fish despite the risks.*

▼ *Alligators are inactive much of the time but can respond very quickly if they sense danger.*

T. Pooley

No safety in numbers

Noise does not stop an alligator or crocodile attack. Victims are often snatched from the middle of large noisy groups of people. In fact, noisy splashing in the water helps the animal to find its prey. Even if other people spear the animal, beat it with sticks, or ram a stick down its throat, a large alligator or crocodile will often not let go of its victim.

Jeff Foott/Auscape International

Saltwater crocodile attacks

An adult saltwater crocodile can grow to 23 feet (7 m) in length and at that huge size has little to fear. Saltwater crocodiles have been responsible for many attacks and deaths among villagers in Southeast Asia, although there are few records available. But records of crocodile attacks have been kept in northern Australia since 1975.

From the evidence of the bodies found after attacks in Australia, most victims of crocodile attacks were taken for food since some or all of their bodies were eaten. Of the crocodiles that attacked human victims, more than half were over 13 feet (4 m) in length but some were as small as 6 feet (2 m).

American alligator attacks in Florida

Early explorers and Indians in Florida were always wary of American alligators, although we now know that they are far less dangerous than Nile or saltwater crocodiles.

In the 1970s it became illegal to hunt alligators in Florida and so there was an increase in the number of alligators in the wild. There was also a large growth in the human population, and many people built homes near the wetland areas where the alligators lived. Because there were so many complaints about nuisance alligators near homes, private trappers were allowed to trap nearly 2,000 alligators. Complaints — and attacks — became less frequent. But in 1986 there were 13 attacks — a record number. It seems possible that alligators that are not hunted or molested in any way are less afraid of and therefore more dangerous to humans.

Alligators and crocodiles, unlike humans, never attack or hunt for "fun". They attack for a reason such as hunger, defense of their family or territory, or in self-defense.

True or false?

Alligators and crocodiles usually eat their fill of fresh meat soon after a kill is made. The idea that an alligator or crocodile will store a victim's body in a lair until the flesh rots or decays is false, although they will sometimes return to a meal they have been unable to eat at one sitting. They also eat fresh corpses they have not killed themselves.

▲ *Newspapers report attacks in the United States and northern Australia. But attacks are more common in more remote areas of Africa and Southeast Asia, where there are no local newspapers to report them.*

Conservation Commission, Northern Territory/Northern Territory News

CONSERVATION COMMISSION

NORTHERN TERRITORY

▲ *By using pictures rather than words, warning signs can be understood by young children and by overseas tourists.*

Better safe than sorry

If you go to an area where alligators or crocodiles are known, there are some precautions you should take.

1. Always pay attention to notices warning of the danger of crocodiles or alligators. You will probably never see an alligator or crocodile but they are there, hidden under the water.
2. If you go on holiday to a new place, always check with local people whether alligators or crocodiles have ever been seen.
3. Do not allow small children or dogs to paddle or wade in the water.
4. Do not think that a shallow pool or even a drainage canal nearby is safe. Alligators and crocodiles sometimes travel some distance from one body of water to another. They can lie hidden in water as shallow as 12 inches (30 cm) for more than an hour.
5. Always stand at least 10 feet (3 m) from the water's edge when fishing. Remember alligators and crocodiles are amphibious and can lunge onto land.
6. Do not gut fish into the water or dump bait into it. These scraps will attract alligators and crocodiles.
7. If you are in a boat, do not dangle your legs or arms in the water.
8. If you see a hatchling alligator or crocodile in the water, leave the area immediately. The adults will probably be close by.
9. Always use a torch when walking near the water's edge at night. The eyes of an alligator or crocodile glow red in a beam of light. But even if you do not see the red eyeshine, be careful! An alligator or crocodile could still be submerged and invisible under a jetty or tree at the water's edge.

Safety screen

When an alligator or crocodile has successfully attacked and killed a victim, it will often return to the same place . . . looking for seconds. Sometimes a barrier of logs and branches can be built in the water to screen off the area and prevent further tragedies.

NO SWIMMING

Jeff Foott/Bruce Coleman Ltd

Jeffrey W. Lang

▶ *In areas where crocodiles are known you may see a crocodile's head above the water (above) or the red eyeshines at night (right), but more often than not you will see nothing until it is too late.*

51

Beliefs and myths

Since the days of ancient Egypt, alligators and crocodiles have had a place in the beliefs of many cultures. In some cultures, alligators or crocodiles have been worshiped and protected as gods. In other cultures they have been seen as sly villains that bring only evil.

The crocodile-god

Sobek, the crocodile-god, was one of the most important gods of ancient Egypt. Sobek had a human body but a crocodile's head. He carried a staff (stick) in his left hand and a symbol of eternity (the ankh) in his right hand.

There were a number of temples built for the worship of Sobek. The most important were at Kom-Ombo and Crocodilopolis. In these temples sacred crocodiles, adorned with gold and precious stones, and with bracelets on their front feet were kept in special pools. When these crocodiles died they were embalmed and mummified. The carcasses were kept in salt baths for two months to dry out the flesh. They were then covered with papyrus leaves and wrapped in perfumed cloth bandages to preserve them. Thousands of mummified adult and newborn crocodiles, and even eggs, have been found locked in special coffins in these ancient temples.

But not all Egyptians worshiped the crocodile-god. At Elephantine on the upper Nile, hunters would beat pigs to make them squeal and lure crocodiles on to hooks — no way to treat a god!

The Chinese dragon

The Chinese proudly see themselves as "descendants of the dragon". Chinese inscriptions from the sixteenth century B.C. show the dragon as a reptile with horns, teeth, and

▲ *The ancient Egyptian god Sobek had a human body but a crocodile's head. The ankh, shaped like a cross, in his right hand showed that he would live for ever.*

◄ *This mummified crocodile was found in a tomb at Kom-Ombo in Upper Egypt.*

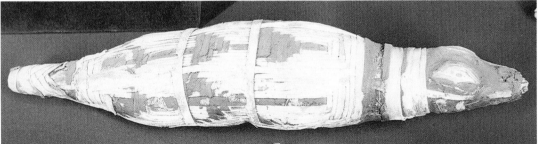

Ronald Sheridan/Ancient Art & Architecture Collection

D. and J. Heaton/Australian Picture Library

Mixed-up beliefs

During the Tang dynasty (A.D. 618–906), the southern Chinese believed they could tell when rain was coming by the alligator's calls. They served alligator meat at weddings since it was a delicacy and was supposed to bring good fortune. The alligator was also a herald of war because of its armor. Being able to prophesy weather and war as well as bringing good fortune made the alligator a very confusing creature.

52

scales. Some Chinese scholars believe that this original dragon was based on the Chinese alligator. Throughout its long history, the mythical Chinese dragon has changed its shape and form, and now looks like a mixture of many animals.

African beliefs
In parts of Africa, crocodiles were worshiped as sacred creatures, just as they were in Egypt. Bobo villagers in the Upper Volta believed that crocodiles were the spirits of the dead protecting the villages where they had once lived. They made food offerings to crocodiles in crocodile-infested pools. Boys were sent to call the crocodiles by name, and each crocodile came only to the boy who called its name.

Up until the nineteenth century, the island of Damba on Lake Victoria in Uganda, was sacred to the crocodiles. The Baganda people threw the bodies of their enemies to the crocodiles there.

In Madagascar crocodiles were even used as judges. A man or woman suspected of a crime was forced to cross a stream full of crocodiles. If the suspect was taken by a crocodile, he or she was obviously guilty!

Ronald Sheridan/Ancient Art & Architecture Collection

▼ *Crocodile hunters in parts of Egypt used pigs tied to stakes to lure crocodiles from the Nile River. As the crocodiles came out of the water to grab the squealing pigs, the hunter killed them with knives and stones.*

Southeast Asia
To many people in the Philippines, the crocodile was the spirit of a previous very fearsome ruler. Crocodiles were therefore not to be killed because the people would suffer a terrible punishment.

In West Timor, up until the late nineteenth century, the princes of Kupang believed that they were descended from crocodiles. They sacrificed beautifully dressed and perfumed young girls as "wives" to the crocodile ancestors.

To the people of Borneo, crocodiles were guardian angels who drove away evil spirits and should be protected. But sometimes it was necessary to kill crocodiles to retrieve the body of a human victim. A sorcerer would stalk crocodile after crocodile slicing open each stomach until he or she found the remains of the child or adult. The villagers then sacrificed a cat to the remaining crocodiles to apologize for the innocent crocodiles they had killed in their search for the "guilty" crocodile.

Australian Aborigines
According to the Gunwinggu tribe of Arnhem Land, the largest river in their area was made by a crocodile ancestor. The crocodile rose behind the mountain ranges and walked toward the sea, chewing the land as it went. The deep furrows it made filled with water to become the Liverpool River.

Whether people believed that alligators and crocodiles were gods, dragons, guardian angels, judges, spirit ancestors, or cruel, crafty animals depended on where and when they lived.

Totems
A totem is an object or animal of special significance to a related group of people and is thought to share a common ancestor with them. A totem must not be harmed and in return it protects the totem group. The Nuer of the Nile valley would wade fearlessly through water containing crocodiles since they knew their totem would not harm them. The Murinbata Aborigines of Australia believed that the Johnston's crocodile was their totemic ancestor Yagpa (old-man crocodile) who protected them. But woe betide anyone who harmed or killed their own totem!

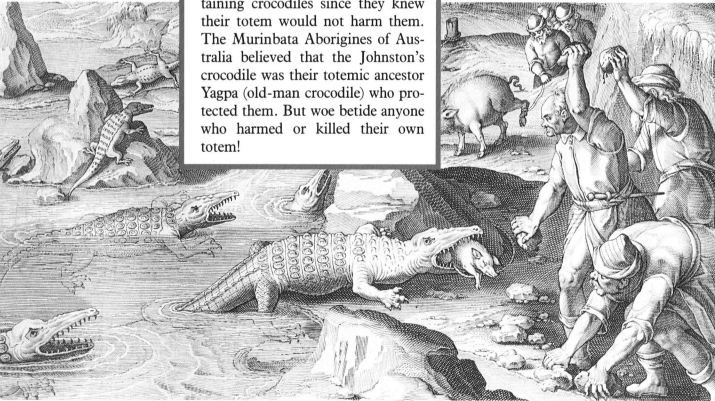

Su Gooders/Ardea London

The artist's view of alligators and crocodiles

Rock art and bark paintings

The earliest picture of what might be a crocodile is an Aboriginal engraving of a huge, scaly beast at Panaramittee in South Australia. The engraving is probably 30,000 years old. Since that time Aboriginal artists have continued to depict crocodiles in their rock art and in bark paintings.

The saltwater crocodile and Johnston's crocodiles are native to northern Australia, and Aboriginal paintings show them as ancestors, totems, predators, or as food.

Paintings

The Egyptians, who had depicted the crocodile as a god in ancient times, came to see the Nile crocodile as another species that shared their environment. Some of their paintings show crocodiles and humans living together almost peacefully.

American paintings were often not as peaceful and certainly the earliest drawing, by the French explorer Le Moyne, shows American Indians and American alligators as deadly enemies.

Alligators and crocodiles became extinct in Europe in prehistoric times. Most Europeans had therefore never seen an alligator or crocodile and it is not surprising that even in paintings of wild animals in the jungle, they usually forgot to include alligators and crocodiles. One of the few European paintings to show a crocodile is Boucher's *Crocodile Hunt*.

Service Historique de la Marine, Paris/Giraudon

▲ *The two very unrealistic alligators in this Amercian picture by the artist Le Moyne do not appear to be putting up much of a struggle against the Indians.*

Cairo Museum/Werner Forman Archive

It is a very confusing painting because the scenery is definitely Egyptian but the hunters all have European faces and the crocodile does not look very realistic.

Sculptures and shields

Villagers on the Sepik River of Papua New Guinea are famous for their carvings, masks, and sculptures of crocodiles. Using wood, shells, beads, feathers, clay, and paint, the villagers still make beautiful artifacts of crocodiles with tattoo-like designs on the heads and bodies, wooden trumpets with crocodile-head mouthpieces, and beautifully painted crocodile shields.

The people of Papua New Guinea have always had a close relationship with their native crocodiles. Some carvings show the crocodile as the original ancestor from which humans, snakes, eels, and fish were born.

▲ Ofo, *a bronze cast of a crocodile, is used in rituals by the Ibo people of Nigeria. The cast itself is a form of homage to the crocodile.*

British Museum (Natural History)/C.M. Dixon

R. Berthold/Australian Picture Library

▲ *This crocodile-headed wooden carving celebrates the belief of some people in Papua New Guinea that the crocodile was the original ancestor, or mother, who gave birth to all humans.*

Keith A.W. Williams/Australasian Nature Transparencies

▲ *For thousands of years Australian Aboriginal artists have included crocodiles in their rock paintings. Saltwater crocodiles and the more harmless Johnston's crocodiles have obviously been living in northern Australia for a long, long time.*

◄ *The ancient Egyptians feared crocodiles but accepted them as part of their world. People believed that after death they would be re-born into a world of fields and rivers just like their own country, as this picture from the* Book of the Dead *shows.*

► *The people on the Sepik River in Papua New Guinea decorate crocodile skulls with colored clay and shells.*

R. Berthold/Australian Picture Library

Skins for sale

All over the world people trade in alligator and crocodile skins. About two million skins are traded each year. In this chapter we shall look at what happens from the time an alligator or crocodile is killed until it appears as a handbag, wallet, or shoes in an exclusive shop in New York, London, Paris or Milan.

▼ *These two hunters use their knives very carefully to make a number of cuts in the skin on the back and legs of a dead crocodile.*

Romulus Whitaker

Skinning and preserving

When hunters have killed an alligator or crocodile in the wild they usually skin it there and then. They lay the dead animal on its belly with its legs stretched out to the side. They stuff dry grass in the snout and cloaca to prevent blood, urine, and feces from escaping. The hunters then make a straight ripping cut, usually down the center of the back from the skull to the tip of the tail. They strip the skin off the limbs and the trunk. They then turn the carcass over onto its back and peel the skin off at the head and tail. In some species the long cut is made down the center of the belly because the skin on the back is of such a high quality that the hunters want it in one piece.

The hunters then rub salt and a preserving agent into the flesh side of the skin. The folded skins are kept in a cooling house until the skin buyers arrive. The skin buyers may pay the hunter as little as $US2–$5 or a bag of sugar for the caiman skin but sell the skins to skin tanners for a great deal more.

Using other parts of the body

Alligator and crocodile meat can be eaten by humans and animals; bones are powdered and added to fertilizers and animal feed; tourists buy teeth and claws made into curios; and the sex organs, musk, and urine are used to make perfume!

▼ *Only in recent years have we begun to understand that crocodiles can behave in subtle and complex ways.*

Australian Picture Library

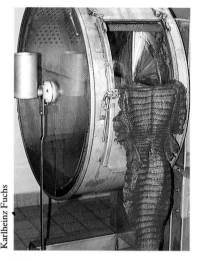

Karlheinz Fuchs

▼▲ *After being dyed in a stainless steel drum (top) the skin or leather is glazed on a special machine (middle) and eventually ends up as a bag like this (bottom).*

Karlheinz Fuchs

How is leather made from raw skin?

Tanneries in France, Italy, Spain, the United States, Japan and the Far East convert the raw skin into leather. There are many different and difficult processes involved in tanning leather.

1. Soaking replaces the water that has been lost during preservation and transport.
2. Liming removes the top layer of skin, called the epidermis, and some of the natural fats.
3. Deliming removes some of the unwanted chemicals, fats, and protein. It reduces the swelling of the greenish-white rubbery skins.
4. Bating cleans the skins further and gets rid of the last of the protein.
5. Pickling takes 8–14 days and dissolves the calcium (found especially in the bony buttons or osteoderms).
6. Tanning in drums of chrome salts converts the hard, horny, pickled hide into soft, flexible leather that does not become rotten and smelly on rewetting.
7. Shaving makes the leather the same thickness all over.
8. Neutralizing removes all the acids that might damage the leather.
9. Retanning with synthetic and vegetable tannins prepares the leather for dyeing.
10. Dyeing gives the leather its color.
11. Fatliquoring gives the dyed leather its softness, stretch, and resistance to tearing.
12. Final finishing gives the leather its feel, gloss, and attractive appearance.

From tannery to the final customer

Tanning the leather is only the first of many stages in producing a handbag. Agents who sell the leather, buyers and import/export companies who get the leather from the tanning country to the handbag-manufacturing country, manufacturers that make the bag, advertisers who advertise the latest fashions, and boutiques that sell the bag are all part of the chain. And they all earn a lot more than a few dollars or a bag of sugar for their efforts! The final customer in the shop may pay $US1,500–$3,000 for a handbag, $600–$800 for a pair of shoes, or $300 for a belt. There are only a few very rich people that can afford these prices.

The future

Many third world countries where alligators or crocodiles are found are now starting their own complete industries. They manage and harvest their native alligators or crocodiles in the wild or in farms and ranches, tan the skins, manufacture the bags, shoes and so on, and export the final goods. Instead of earning very little money by selling off the untreated skins from their native species, they will be able to employ far more people, earn higher profits, and improve the economy of their countries.

Throughout the world those involved in the skin trade now realize that there is not an unlimited supply of alligators and crocodiles. Hunters, skin buyers, farmers and ranchers, tanners, import/export companies, fashion designers, and manufacturers are beginning to work with wildlife law-enforcement agencies, scientists, and conservationists to preserve the world's alligators and crocodiles.

Karlheinz Fuchs

▶ *As well as using pieces of skin to make bags and shoes, claws and head are made into keyrings, ornaments, or souvenirs.*

L.C. Marigo/Bruce Coleman Ltd

C.B. Frith/Bruce Coleman Ltd

Peter Brazaitis

C.B. Frith/Bruce Coleman Ltd

Hunters and hunting

Throughout history, people who lived near alligators and crocodiles hunted them occasionally for food, medicine, or religious purposes. But in the nineteenth century, when European colonies were set up in remote parts of the world, commercial hunting of alligators and crocodiles, for their skins and for profits, began in earnest.

Peter Beard

Hunting in Africa

In 1869 an article in the *Natal Herald* said that "the skin of the monsters was suitable for ladies' boots". Hunters who had been hunting other animals such as elephants for their ivory, then turned to hunting crocodiles. By the 1950s, 60,000 Nile crocodile skins were exported each year from East Africa alone. It was not until the late 1960s that Nile crocodiles were given some protection from hunters.

Hunting in India and neighboring countries

Hunter-gatherer tribes were paid by skin dealers to hunt for crocodiles. A number of different hunting methods were used. Hunters caught crocodiles with baited hooks, with nets submerged in the water near the crocodiles' basking sites, with harpoons, and with guns. Hunters in Pakistan would even dive into lakes or crawl into the crocodiles' burrows to attach ropes to the muggers hiding there.

There are no records of how many crocodiles — or foolhardy hunters — died.

Julian A. Dimock/Department of Library Services. American Museum of Natural History

Hunting in the United States

Commercial hunting of American alligators reached a peak during and immediately after the American Civil War (1861–65). Alligator skins were used to make boots, shoes, traveling bags, saddlebags, belts, and other items. By the early 1900s, alligator skin was even used to cover books and chairs.

When the skin buyers could not get enough alligator skins they looked for crocodile and caiman skins from other countries such as South and Central America, Africa, and Asia.

Hunting in South America

Large-scale commercial hunting of caimans in South America began in the 1950s. Black caimans, whose skins were the most valuable, were hunted almost to extinction. The hunters therefore began hunting the bony and less valuable common caimans. Common caimans are still hunted in South America and make up 60 percent of all skins traded worldwide today. Many of these skins are hunted illegally by poor peasants who hunt at night from canoes with harpoons and lights. They earn little money, unlike the smugglers who buy the skins and export them to countries all over the world, often with false documents.

▶ *Despite its bony, less valuable skin the common caiman is hunted more than any other species, mainly because there are so many of them (that is, they are "common").*

The best skins

The most valuable skins come from saltwater crocodiles, Nile crocodiles, and Siamese crocodiles. These species have small scales and no osteoderms in the belly as in this picture. The skins from bonier species, like caimans, are less valuable, and dishonest dealers often pretend they are the skins from valuable species. Few people can tell the difference.

S.C. Bisserot

American Indians (far left), tribes in Africa (top), and the natives of Papua New Guinea (below) used to hunt a small number of alligators or crocodiles as food for their families. In the late nineteenth century, skin buyers began to offer money for the skins and hunting increased dramatically.

Busy hunters

It is very difficult to get figures on how many alligators and crocodiles were shot in the past, but the diaries of a few hunters suggest the number was very high. Hunters in the United States would kill up to 42 alligators in a single night and one hunter could kill 800 alligators in a single season. A Scot, called Tshaywa-ing wenya ("He who kills crocodiles") by the natives, killed almost 300 crocodiles in Africa in three years. Percy Jackson, another hunter, killed 1,300 crocodiles in 20 years – and he was only a part-time hunter.

Romulus Whitaker

Farming and ranching

In the 1960s, many people involved in the skin trade realized that raising alligators and crocodiles in captivity might be a better way to ensure a constant supply of skins than hunting them in the wild. Governments and conservationists thought that farming and ranching might help to protect endangered species. In this chapter we shall look at how alligators and crocodiles are raised, just like other animals, in farms and ranches.

▲ *This female is nesting in her own private stall on a crocodile farm.*

Collecting and incubating eggs

Ranchers collect eggs from the wild some time after they are laid, since they are less likely to be damaged than newly laid eggs. The ranchers go to known breeding areas and follow the females' tracks to the nests. They open the nests and mark each egg as it is removed so that it can be packed in the same position as it was in the nest. The eggs are packed into boxes (often of styrofoam) and protected by packing material. The eggs are then taken back to incubators on the ranch.

On farms, which have incubators near where the females lay, eggs are collected as soon after laying as possible. They can even be collected as the female is actually laying them since she is quite docile at that time.

The eggs are incubated at controlled temperatures in hothouses, in styrofoam boxes, or in open trays.

▼ *Eggs are carefully collected from a gharial's nest to be taken back to a ranch for incubation.*

Q. What is the difference between a farm and a ranch?

A. Ranches take eggs, hatchlings, and even adult alligators and crocodiles from the wild and rear them in captivity until they are of skinning size. Farms raise all their stock from eggs laid by females on the farm. They do not take eggs, hatchlings or adults from the wild.

▲ *Eggs are hatched at controlled temperatures in hothouses.*

▲ *This villager in Papua New Guinea keeps live young crocodiles in a home-made pen until the local ranch collects them.*

▼ *A box trap is easy to set, but a very large alligator can injure itself by thrashing against the wire sides.*

Rearing hatchlings

Rearing hatchlings in captivity is not easy. If they are kept in outside ponds, many die from diseases caused by the changes in the outside temperature. Many farms now raise hatchlings in hothouses where the temperature is constant. They grow more rapidly and remain healthier than those raised outside.

After the first year, hatchlings are either moved to outside ponds or continue to live in the hothouses.

Breeding

Farms raise their own breeding stock on the farm, but ranches often get their adult breeding stock from the wild. Breeding stock, on farms and ranches, are held in pens with ponds large enough and deep enough to allow for mating.

Many farms and ranches put only one male into a pond with a number of breeding females so that the male can concentrate on breeding, not fighting with other males. Some farms and ranches also use a separate nesting stall for each female to stop them fighting over nest sites. The stalls can also be closed off to make it easier for staff to collect the eggs without being attacked by the female.

Q. How do you drug an alligator or crocodile?

A. Very carefully! A hand-held syringe is too dangerous — no alligator or crocodile caught in a trap would lie still to let a human near enough to use it. Dart guns are not safe either since the darts might bounce off the animal's armor and strike the handlers nearby. A long pole with a syringe attached is used to inject the tranquilizing drug into the tail.

Capturing adults from the wild

Capturing an unwilling large alligator or crocodile without injuring it is a difficult task! Ranchers catch adult alligators or crocodiles in a rope net, box trap, or a Pitman trap.

But catching the animal is only the first step. The next step is to release the animal from the trap and transport it to the ranch. The alligator or crocodile is given a tranquilizing drug. It can still see, hear, smell, and feel pain so its jaws are usually taped together and its eyes covered for the journey back to the ranch.

The methods of capturing and drugging are constantly being improved. The main aims are to avoid stress and injury to the animal — and the handlers.

Killing and skinning

When a crocodile or alligator reaches skinning size it is killed humanely by shooting in the head or by severing the spinal cord. Skinning is done immediately by skilled skinners.

The benefits of farms and ranches

On farms and ranches, alligators and crocodiles can be studied by scientists much more easily than in the wild. Scientists have learned a great deal about the life cycle of alligators and crocodiles from their studies on captive animals.

The chances of survival of eggs, hatchlings, and even adults are much better in captivity than in the wild for a number of reasons. Nest and incubation temperatures can be controlled on farms and ranches, and predators can be kept away. Animals in captivity mature and breed earlier, build more nests, and lay more eggs than those in the wild.

One of the main advantages of farming and ranching, however, is that it cuts down the amount of hunting — legal and illegal — of wild alligators and crocodiles. This is good news for conservationists, skin buyers . . . and wild alligators and crocodiles.

▲ *These Nile crocodiles have been raised in captivity at a farm in Zimbabwe.*

Farms and ranches around the world

E.A. McIlhenny, a successful businessman, donated large areas of marshlands in Florida as a wildlife area. This land became a giant alligator ranch, and on part of the land, Rockefeller Wildlife Refuge was created. At the Refuge researchers investigated the best pen size, diet, sex ratio, and number of alligators required for raising healthy alligators on ranches and farms. The results of this research are now being used by farms and ranches around the world.

Africa

In 1965 Zimbabwe became the first African country to start crocodile ranches. The government supported the ranches since hunting of Nile crocodiles had reduced their numbers dramatically. Ten years later the first two ranches, on Lake Kariba, found that keeping their own egg-laying females was more efficient than collecting eggs from the wild, so the ranches became farms. There are now ten farms in Zimbabwe, and crocodile farms are also operating in Kenya, Tanzania, Zambia, South Africa, Mozambique, and Madagascar.

Australia

Edward River Crocodile Farm was the first Australian crocodile farm. Its main aims are to conserve young saltwater crocodiles and to provide employment for the local Aboriginal community. There are now three other crocodile farms in Queensland.

There are also three crocodile ranches in the Northern Territory of Australia. These ranches are allowed to take saltwater crocodile eggs and Johnston's crocodile hatchlings from the wild for rearing on the ranches.

These Australian farms and ranches earn money from tourists or from selling crocodile skins and meat.

Madras Crocodile Bank, India

Madras Crocodile Bank, South of Madras in India, is a conservation or educational farm that protects and breeds endangered species. It also gives scientists the opportunity to conduct research and gives the public information on alligators and crocodiles.

Madras Crocodile Bank breeds muggers and nine other species of alligators and crocodiles, some of which have already been or will be released back into the wild.

Papua New Guinea

Mainland Holdings Crocodile Farm and Ranch at Lae in Papua New Guinea buys live wild crocodiles from smallholder farmers and hunters. The money these farmers and hunters earn from selling live crocodiles means there is no need for them to kill the crocodiles.

When a new crocodile arrives at the ranch, it is given a health check and is placed in the "hospital" if it is suffering from disease or spear wounds.

The ranch has its own poultry farm that can feed up to 40,000 crocodiles although, at present, there are only 28,500 crocodiles of all ages and sizes on the ranch.

Farming and ranching alligators and crocodiles is a new type of farming and is no more dangerous than farming other livestock — although the "farm animals" are a little unusual.

▲ The Samut Prakan Crocodile Farm, near Bangkok in Thailand, is popular with tourists for its "crocodile-wrestling" shows; but it has also helped to save Thailand's Siamese crocodiles from extinction.

An alligator palace

American alligators at Rockefeller Wildlife Refuge are reared in special hothouses where temperature, humidity (dampness), diet, disease, and space for individual alligators can be controlled. The hothouses even have piped music so that the alligators will not be disturbed by outside noises. Under these conditions alligators grow to more than 3 feet (1 m) in one year — much bigger than they would grow in one year in the wild.

Bill Green

▲ This saltwater crocodile has been caught in a rope trap before being taken to one of Australia's ranches.

Romulus Whitaker

▲ *In 1969 Edward River Crocodile Farm in Queensland, Australia had 600 crocodiles. Now it has 7,800 crocodiles*

▶ *This young boy in Papua New Guinea will be paid more money for a wild crocodile alive than dead. This encourages villagers not to kill smaller crocodiles for their skins.*

Bill Green

Protecting alligators and crocodiles

Conservationists may only now be winning the battle to protect alligators and crocodiles. Some species that were once endangered are now out of danger, and there is now much less illegal hunting. But there are still species close to extinction, and there are still illegal hunters and skin dealers around.

No protection

Until the 1970s, there was no international protection for alligators and crocodiles. Each year 5–10 million alligators and crocodiles were killed for their skins.

When countries with native wild alligators and crocodiles realized that these animals were a source of income that would soon die out without protection, they began to pass laws. Some countries banned the hunting of all native alligators or crocodiles. Others protected the animals in parts of the country where they were scarce but allowed hunting to continue in parts of the country where they were still abundant.

Unfortunately, traders found ways to get around these laws by smuggling skins from protected areas into unprotected areas or into countries where hunting was still legal. Once the skins reached a legal area they could be shipped anywhere in the world.

The rich countries that bought illegal skins believed that it was not their job to stop the trade in illegal hides — it was up to the countries selling the skins to stop illegal hunting.

Protection at last

As early as 1900, United States Congressman John Lacey had pointed out that to stop illegal trade in wildlife it is necessary to make both the buyers and the sellers responsible. Based on his ideas, the United States passed a law in 1969 that not only protected wildlife within the United States but also organized a conference to draw up an international treaty on endangered species. In 1973, in Washington D.C., 81 nations drew up the Convention on International Trade in Endangered Species of Wild Fauna and Flora (known as CITES, for short).

▼ *Papua New Guinea now protects its native crocodiles but allows skin buyers, like the family shown here, to buy and sell a small number of legal skins each year.*

◀ *Unfortunately, as the remains of these Johnston's crocodiles show, poachers still hunt illegally and sell the skins to smugglers.*

Endangered!

Seventeen of the 22 species of alligators and crocodiles are endangered in all or some of the countries where they are found. They are in danger of extinction from hunting, loss of habitat, collection of their eggs, or from interbreeding with other species. Many species are not properly protected in national parks and there are not enough of them being reared on farms and ranches to ensure that the species does not disappear . . . for ever.

▲ *A saltwater crocodile makes its escape as soon as researchers have finished measuring and tagging it. The tag will help to protect it from poachers.*

CITES lists endangered species on two lists called Appendix I and Appendix II. Appendix I lists endangered species that may not be traded internationally. Appendix II lists species that are not at present endangered but that might become so if trade is not controlled. All species of alligators and crocodiles are listed on Appendix I or Appendix II.

How protection works

All nations signing the treaty must keep records of all protected wildlife imported (brought into the country) or exported (sent out of the country). This means that even if illegal skins can be smuggled out of one country, their arrival in the country buying them will be reported. CITES also encourages countries to print export permits on security paper (like banknotes) that is difficult to forge or alter, and to use plastic tags (that cannot be removed) on legal hides.

By these means CITES nations can now spot and stop more illegal skins than ever before. Unfortunately, despite all their efforts, illegal skins still get through.

How the smugglers operate

CITES can only encourage, not force, nations to use self-locking tags on legal hides. Many caiman skins from South America are not tagged. Illegal skin dealers or smugglers may export a mixed shipment of skin pieces from a number of legal and illegal sources. Several pieces from animals of different species and from different countries may be used to make a handbag. The skin or leather may be shipped through a number of different countries before it reaches the final destination. All of this makes sorting out the legal from the illegal skins very difficult.

Smugglers often bribe officials to give them false documents or they lie about the species being exported or the country from which it came. It is only when the shipment arrives, for example in the United States, that it might be seized and confiscated as illegal. By that time it is too late for the caimans that have been killed illegally — or for the United States importer who has already paid a lot of money for what he or she thought were legal skins.

Hope for the future

By 1980, world trade in alligator and crocodile skins had dropped to 1.5–2 million skins, of which about one half were illegal skins exported from southern South America. Now, for the first time, the number of skins will probably be less than 1 million and, if protection methods continue to improve, most of these will be legal skins.

Q. Why are so many common caiman skins sold?

A. There are more common caimans than any other species. The problems of the bony osteoderms in their bellies has been overcome in two ways. Hunters often throw away the belly skin and save only the *chalecos* — the soft throat and strips from the flanks. Improved tanning processes can also solve (or dissolve!) the bony problem.

CITES Appendix I (endangered species, trade illegal)	CITES Appendix II (not at present endangered, trade controlled)
Chinese alligator	American alligator
black caiman	common caiman (some subspecies)
common caiman (some subspecies)	Cuvier's dwarf caiman
broad-snouted caiman	Schneider's dwarf caiman
American crocodile	African slender-snouted crocodile (from Congo only)
African slender-snouted crocodile (from all countries except Congo)	Johnston's crocodile
Orinoco crocodile	Nile crocodile (from 11 African countries)
Morelet's crocodile	New Guinea crocodile
Nile crocodile (from all countries not listed on Appendix II)	saltwater crocodile (from Australia, Papua New Guinea, and Indonesia)
Philippine crocodile	dwarf crocodile (from Congo only)
mugger	
saltwater crocodile (from all countries not listed on Appendix II)	
Cuban crocodile	
Siamese crocodile	
dwarf crocodile (from all countries except Congo)	
false gharial	
gharial	

▲ *With locked plastic tags on their tails, these American alligators can be easily identified as legally hunted.*

65

Glossary

AMPHIBIOUS — Able to live on both land and water. Although you may be able to swim, you are not amphibious because you cannot live, eat, sleep and breed in the water.

BASK — To lie in the warmth of the sun. You bask when you sunbathe in summer.

CARNIVORES — Mammals that eat flesh or meat. Humans are carnivores, although vegetarians choose not to be.

CLOACA — One single vent or opening through which eggs, urine, and feces pass out of an animal. Birds, reptiles, many fish, and some mammals have a cloaca.

CLUTCH — A number of eggs laid and hatched at the same time; a nestful of eggs.

CONSERVATION — The attempt to keep the environment and the plants and animals in it from perishing or becoming damaged.

COURTING — Spending time with and paying attention to a member of the opposite sex, with the aim of finding a mate.

ESTUARIES — Wide river mouths formed where rivers reach the sea.

EVOLUTION — The development of animals over thousands or millions of years with gradual changes to the body to suit new conditions.

EXTINCT — Having come to an end or died out as a species. When the last living animal in a species dies, the species becomes extinct.

FOOD CHAIN — A series of plants, insects, and animals that are connected by their feeding habits. The smallest (for example, an insect) is eaten by a larger animal (for example, a fish) that, in turn, is eaten by an even larger animal (for example, an alligator).

GHARA — A Hindi (Indian) word meaning mud pot used to describe the very unusual large round knob on the snout of male gharials.

GIZZARD — A muscular stomach that grinds large lumps of food into small pieces or particles.

GLANDS — Organs or tissues in the body that discharge a chemical substance that is either used somewhere else in the body (secretion) or passed out of the body (excretion).

HABITAT — The place, such as fresh water, warm seas, or mountain tops, where an animal or plant naturally lives. The habitat provides the right environment and food supplies for the animal to survive.

INCUBATING — Hatching (eggs) by keeping them warm either by sitting on them (like birds), covering them with nesting material (like alligators and crocodiles), or using artificial means (like hothouses on ranches and farms).

INTERBREED — To breed with a different species of animal in captivity (animals almost never interbreed in the wild).

OSTEODERMS — Bony buttons embedded (stuck) in the skin. The word is made up from the Greek word *osteo-* meaning bone and the Latin word *dermis* meaning skin.

POIKILOTHERMIC — "Cold-blooded;" having a body temperature that goes up and down according to the temperature of the environment. Humans are not poikilothermic since the temperature of a healthy human body stays at 98.4°F (37°C) whatever the weather.

PREDATORS	Animals (including humans) that survive by preying on or catching other animals for food.
PREY	The animal that is caught and eaten by a predator.
RAINFOREST	Thick forest, mainly in the tropics, that has heavy rainfall all year and is usually very damp.
REPTILES	A class of animals that crawl without legs (like snakes) or on very short legs (like alligators, crocodiles, lizards, and turtles).
SECONDARY BONY PALATE	An extra or second palate made of three bones in the roof of the mouth. This palate separates the mouth from the breathing passages.
SCALES	Thin, flat, horny or hard palates covering the skin of some animals such as fish, snakes, alligators, and crocodiles.
SCUTES	Large scales or plates on alligator and crocodile backs and tails that stick up or out to the side instead of lying flat against the body like other scales.
SPECIES	A group of animals whose bodies share common features. There are thousands of different species of animals, but only members of the same species can breed and produce offspring that will be able to have babies of their own when they grow up.
SUBMERGED	Completely or almost completely under the water.
THECODONTIANS	Members of a large and very varied group of fossil animals from which alligators, crocodiles, birds, dinosaurs, and many other extinct groups evolved.
TROPICS	The hot regions or countries near the equator and between the tropic of Cancer (to the north) and the tropic of Capricorn (to the south).
VERTEBRATES	Animals, including humans, that have a spine or backbone made up of small bones called vertebrae (singular — vertebra).

List of scientific names

Common name	Scientific name
African slender-snouted crocodile	*Crocodylus cataphractus*
American alligator	*Alligator mississippiensis*
American crocodile	*Crocodylus acutus*
black caiman	*Melanosuchus niger*
broad-snouted caiman	*Caiman latirostris*
Chinese alligator	*Alligator sinensis*
common caiman	*Caiman crocodilus*
Cuban crocodile	*Crocodylus rhombifer*
Cuvier's dwarf caiman	*Paleosuchus palpebrosus*
dwarf crocodile	*Osteolaemus tetraspis*
false gharial	*Tomistoma schlegelii*
gharial	*Gavialis gangeticus*
Johnston's crocodile	*Crocodylus johnsoni*
Morelet's crocodile	*Crocodylus moreletii*
mugger	*Crocodylus palustris*
New Guinea crocodile	*Crocodylus novaeguineae*
Nile crocodile	*Crocodylus niloticus*
Orinoco crocodile	*Crocodylus intermedius*
Philippine crocodile	*Crocodylus mindorensis*
saltwater crocodile	*Crocodylus porosus*
Schneider's dwarf caiman	*Paleosuchus trigonatus*
Siamese crocodile	*Crocodylus siamensis*

Oliver Strewe/Wildlight Photo Agency

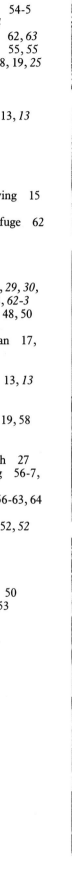

William E. Magnusson

Dieter and Mary Plage/Bruce Coleman Ltd

Jack Green/Australian Nature Photographs